Patricia Magnano Madsen
33c Hackthorne Road
Cashmere, Christchurch 2
New Zealand   eMail: MTflyfisher@netaccess.co.nz   PH: (03) 337-9370

Monday, February 2, 1998

Dear Gary,

Per our conversation before leaving the states in September, please find enclosed our book, "NEW ZEALAND'S TOP TROUT FISHING WATERS". We feel our book has much to offer the angler planning a fishing adventure in New Zealand.

Our guide book differs from others in that the co-authors live and fish 6 months in each country and address the differences in NZ fishing versus US

Kate —
A real how — to, where — to. If possible, I'd like to keep the book. G

Island and South Island depending on length of stay and the listed the contact information for transport, accommodation, fly shops, registered guides etc.

We appreciate your interest in reviewing it. Should you require any additional information we can be contacted at the above address until 1 April or at:

    P.O.Box 1963
    Great Falls, Montana 59803-1963
    (406) 761-6313, FAX: (406) 453-3540
    eMail: MTflyfisher@worldnet.att.net 7 April - 1 October

Sincerely,

John Kent
Patti Magnano Madsen

NEW ZEALAND'S TOP
TROUT FISHING WATERS

New Zealand's Top Trout Fishing Waters

John Kent
Patti Magnano Madsen

REED

Published 1997 by Reed Books, a division of Reed Publishing (NZ) Ltd, 39 Rawene Road, Birkenhead, Auckland. Associated companies, branches and representatives throughout the world.

Text and photographs © John Kent and Patti Magnano Madsen 1997

ISBN 0 79000590 5
Cover design by Michele Stutton
Cover photograph by David Hallett
Designed by Graeme Leather

Printed in New Zealand

CONTENTS

FOREWORD

*'So long as water moves, so long as fins press against it,
so long as weather changes and man is fallible, fish
will remain in some measure unpredictable. And so
long as there is unpredictability, there will be luck, both
good and bad.'*

RODERICK HAIG-BROWN
Measure of the Year

Allow me to add — So long as there is unpredictability there
will be — adventure! With its thousands of miles of clear,
free flowing and undammed rivers; with its hundreds of
pristine lakes; with its wild unplanted trout; with its extre-
mely challenging fishing situations; with its tiny human
population and lack of industry; with one of the safest and
loveliest settings on this planet — yes, with all this and more
— New Zealand is home to our finest fishing adventures.

There are always those zealots who guard their fishing
destinations with a vengeance; who believe that 'others'
equate to too many people in their fishing hole; who believe
our sport suffers from too many new anglers and who would
happily do away with all education and fishing references. I
must confess that there are times in my fly fishing clinics
when the thought of directing certain students to something
like billiards or bowling is most appealing. Fortunately that
is not true of Patti and John, the authors of this excellent
reference.

It is highly unlikely that any angler ever has or ever will,
for that matter, explore all of the fishing possibilities that
exist in this South Pacific paradise. These two highly
dedicated fly fishers have come a lot closer than most and
are doing their damnedest to fish them all. They are highly
social and willing to share most of their discoveries, knowing
that only in numbers and unity can we conserve our waters

and that solitude is but a short walk away on most waters. You are lucky indeed to have found this book. I hope it will lead you to your own fishing adventure, perhaps even a fishing fairy tale.

MEL KRIEGER

INTRODUCTION

There are over 700 rivers and 200 lakes in New Zealand worth fishing. New Zealand is a fly angler's paradise as most rivers and lakes have excellent water quality and offer sight fishing to large wild brown and rainbow trout. There is virtually no private water and the licence fees are reasonable. Access to most rivers and lakes is easy and there are wilderness areas providing trophy trout for the adventurous. Many overseas anglers visiting New Zealand have limited time to fish and the wide range of water available can be confusing and overwhelming. This book has been written to make that choice easier and to offer tips on fishing New Zealand waters.

We have carefully chosen our top spots but understand there are many others equally as good. To simplify the angler's itinerary we have endeavoured to group these fishing spots in close proximity to a central location so you have a choice of rivers and lakes to visit within a reasonable travelling distance. We have also included information on the availability of local fishing guides and fly shops in the vicinity. And, to be well entertained on non-fishing days, various local attractions have also been mentioned.

It has been our pleasure to have fished the top spots described and we hope this guide book will direct you to what we consider an angler's eldorado and that you will share in our delight.

PLANNING A TRIP
TO NEW ZEALAND

GENERAL

New Zealand's three main islands lie in the South Pacific between latitude 34°S and 47°S. These volcanic islands sit astride the boundary between the Indian-Australian and Pacific Plates hence earthquake and volcanic eruptions are not uncommon. The altitude ranges from sea level to 3764 metres at Mt Cook. New Zealand is a long, narrow, windy country, being 1600 km long and 400 km wide at its maximum breadth. Total land area is similar to the state of Montana. New Zealand was first populated 800–1200 years ago by Polynesian voyagers and it was not until 150 years ago that European colonisation began. The country's present total population is 3.6 million, two thirds of whom live in the North Island. Maori comprise twelve percent of the present population with the majority living in the North Island. A large Polynesian population (non-Maori) also reside in New Zealand with the vast majority living in the largest city, Auckland. The common language is English.

CLIMATE

New Zealand has a mild oceanic-type climate. A mixture of anti-cyclones and depressions, modified by the topography, produces a variable weather pattern often difficult to forecast. Much of the country receives over 2000 hours of sunshine per year. The prevailing westerly winds hit the Southern Alps and shed their moisture leading to wide differences in rainfall. Parts of the West Coast of the South Island receive up to 6000 mm of rain annually with 8000 mm in the alps. On the eastern side of the alps in areas of Central Otago, rainfall can be as low as 300 mm per year. With a constantly changing weather pattern significant characteristics of each district's climate will be detailed in the text.

PASSPORT AND VISA

A current passport must be carried and a visa may be required for stays longer than three months; the maximum stay permitted is six months.

CUSTOMS REGULATIONS ON ENTRY

The Ministry of Agriculture and Fisheries does not allow raw materials to be brought into the country. Flies, waders and boots may need inspection. If fumigation is required items may be held by the Ministry for approximately one week. Delivery will be made if an address is given, otherwise one must personally arrange to pick the items up at the Ministry office. It is advisable to thoroughly wash and clean waders and boots before arrival.

BANKING SYSTEM

The currency is dollars and cents, and banks and money exchanges are readily available in all cities and many towns. Major credit cards are also acceptable in most places and full legal and commercial services are easily accessible.

HEALTH SYSTEM

It is advisable to carry health insurance as injury by accident is only partially covered by the Accident Compensation Corporation. There are excellent medical and dental services available should these be needed.

CITIES

Auckland, in the north of the North Island, is by far the largest city with greater Auckland having a population in excess of one million. Your first port of call will usually be the Auckland International Airport. Wellington, at the southern end of the North Island, is the capital city and houses a democratically elected government. Christchurch and Dunedin are the South Island's main cities. Smaller cities and country towns also provide unique opportunities and facilities for the tourist angler.

AUCKLAND

Auckland, New Zealand's largest and most cosmopolitan city, lies across a narrow isthmus between the Waitemata and Manukau harbours. Auckland's main street, Queen Street, leads to the waterfront and from here, ferries and pleasure craft offer access to the Hauraki Gulf Maritime Park and its many beautiful islands. This vibrant city has numerous cafes, restaurants, art galleries and shopping malls to explore and enjoy. The city is dotted with extinct volcanic cones and these provide easy landmarks for the visitor. There are numerous parks and gardens while the North Shore across the Harbour Bridge is blessed with many safe beaches. If one is spending a few days in Auckland, then we suggest visiting Kelly Tarlton's Underwater Centre, the Auckland Museum and cafe, the Auckland Art Gallery, the Sky Tower and casino and, if the weather is favourable, taking a cruise on the harbour and Hauraki Gulf.

For more information, contact the Auckland Visitor Centre at 299 Queen Street.

CHRISTCHURCH

Christchurch, the South Island's largest city, has been described as the most English city outside England. It is known as the Garden City and a walk through the Botanical Gardens and Hagley Park or along the banks of the Avon

River should not be missed. There are excellent cafes and restaurants and good shopping. The Antarctic Centre at the airport is well worth visiting and a ride on the gondola to the top of the Port Hills unveils superb views of the city, Lyttelton Harbour, the Canterbury Plains and the Southern Alps. Take the tram to the Arts Centre located in the elegant stone Gothic Revival buildings where there are theatres, craft studios, cafes and shops. Across Rolleston Avenue from the Arts Centre is the Canterbury Museum. More information can be obtained from the Visitor Centre in Oxford Terrace opposite Noah's Hotel.

TRANSPORT

Internal air links to other population centres are easy and reliable but rather expensive. Bus service is reasonable and rail links only the main cities. Campervans and cars are readily hired but need to be booked prior to the Christmas holiday season (mid-December to mid-February). Rental agencies do not charge drop fees and provide maps. Vehicles in New Zealand are right-hand drive and the English system of driving on the left side of the road is operable. New Zealanders have a reputation for being aggressive drivers and on the limited motorway system you may be passed on either side. Most roads are single lane and country roads are often unsealed. An international driver's licence is not required by drivers from countries using the Roman alphabet. However, visitors from countries using characters will need an international licence.

An inter-island ferry provides sea transport between the North and the South Island; this ship also carries vehicles. It is important to book at least two months prior to the high holiday season. Crossings take about three and a half hours.

The Automobile Association does not recommend buying a vehicle and selling it at the end of the trip unless you plan an extended holiday of two to three months. 'Buyer beware' was their advice.

Maps

Road maps can be purchased from the Automobile Association, book stores and some service stations or may be provided by the campervan and rental car operators. More detailed maps can be bought from Land Information New Zealand (formerly the Department of Survey and Land Information) who have offices in the main city centres.

Accommodation

There is a wide range of accommodation available in New Zealand but only the major cities offer luxury first class hotels. Camping grounds, cabins, backpackers' hostels, homestays, bed and breakfasts, farmstays, motels (most with cooking and laundry facilities), lodges and hotels offer an extensive selection and diverse experience. Hotels, unless specified as luxury hotels, could be anything from a country pub with rooms to a tavern with no accommodation.

Food

We suggest grocery shopping at the supermarkets where a wide selection of items is available. Corner dairies (convenience stores) supply limited groceries at higher prices but remain open for longer hours. Pharmacies (drug stores) do not sell food. The larger cities offer good restaurants but prices tend to be high. However, tipping is not the social custom. Entrées are not the main course and most items are à la carte. Tap water can be safely drunk but it is wise to filter or boil water taken from streams and rivers.

Shopping

Information relating to fly shops will be detailed under each district although the main city centres generally have the best selection. For non-fishing days there are many craft

Rough West Coast accommodation

shops, galleries and antique stores to visit and often the most interesting are found tucked away in the smallest of townships.

ELECTRICITY

New Zealand's power supply is 230–240 volts. Most hotels and motels provide 110 volt AC sockets for razors only. An adaptor or converter will be required. Power outlets accept only flat two- or three-pin plugs.

PUBLIC HOLIDAYS

Many facilities close on public holidays although some shops now remain open. Public holidays include:

Christmas Day	December 25
Boxing Day	December 26
New Year's Day	January 1, and also January 2
Waitangi Day	February 6
Easter	late March-April
Anzac Day	April 25
Queen's Birthday	first Monday in June
Labour Day	fourth Monday in October

There are also provincial holidays, and Christmas school holidays extend from late December until early February.

Unique features of New Zealand Fishing

New Zealand fishing is magical, seductive, challenging and more captivating than fishing in the USA for a variety of reasons. It requires different skills and a more thoughtful approach. Local weather patterns must be checked daily or well-laid fishing plans could prove futile. Flexibility and local knowledge are of utmost importance. River and stream selection may need altering on the day because of wind or weather conditions. First-time anglers would be well advised to contact and hire local professional guides in each region.

A prerequisite for successfully fishing New Zealand waters is a good solid command of casting skills and a rod that meets the demands of windy conditions, longer tippets, weighted nymphs and streamside vegetation. Early season results are often measured by the weight of nymphs one can comfortably cast. To consistently make an accurate first cast is vital for good results. A well-known New Zealand guide has stated there is an 80 percent chance of hooking a sighted fish on the first cast but the odds drop to 20 percent by the fourth. In addition, optimum water temperatures on average tend to be much cooler than experienced in the States. On occasion we have found fish rising to a dry fly in water measured at 11°C (52°F).

Tippets are comparatively heavier than most anglers use in the USA but limp enough for a good drift. As well, the tippet must be stiff enough to turn over in windy conditions and strong enough to handle good-sized trout with some authority.

The water clarity in New Zealand is exceptional and because the trout population is not high in most waters, spotting and stalking fish is the preferred technique on many rivers and lakes. This can be a difficult technique to master and the use of a professional guide to help with this aspect of fishing is invaluable, especially for the first-time visiting angler. Good Polaroids and the ability to 'read the water' are essential. Blind casting spooks more fish than one realises. As there may be only one fish in a run or pool, spotting that fish before casting is critical for a hook up. Even though heavily fished rivers present us with 'educated trout' that are difficult to seduce even with the smallest morsel, wilderness rivers rarely visited by an angler can be equally as difficult. The slightest variation in normal surroundings such as line shadow, jerky streamside movements, wading bow waves and body scent create enough disturbance to make the trout wary. There are exceptions to spotting and stalking and these include winter fishing in the Rotorua and Taupo districts, float tube or boat fishing, and stream mouth and night fishing.

Clothing that blends with the environment, keeping a low profile, and a stealthy approach enable the angler to move closer to a fish, thereby improving the accuracy of the cast. Use streamside vegetation as a camouflage and remember that trout have more difficulty seeing you when the sun is behind you. If there is glare on the water try crossing to the other side and make use of trees and scrub to minimise light reflection. Camouflage clothing can be worn but is unnecessary in our opinion. Any dull browns, fawns, blues and greens are satisfactory. Avoid red, white and yellow.

Boots and shorts are worn for wet wading most rivers as a lot of walking is usually required. Heavy neoprene waders are fine for lake, stream mouth, winter or night fishing but become hot and cumbersome for back country rivers. Lightweight waders can easily be damaged by thorny scrub. Felt soles are very useful when wading some rivers but can be dangerous when traversing steep tussock hillsides.

Whereas the best hatches occur in the USA on calm, misty and cloudy days, calm sunny days are the best in New Zealand. Spotting fish takes precedence over hatch blizzards. The ultraviolet light intensity is high so protection creams and lip salve are a necessity.

To successfully fish most New Zealand rivers in summer, fitness and endurance are important. Good access to back country streams can be limited and long days tramping and walking rivers are often necessary. Being physically fit makes fishing in New Zealand much more enjoyable.

Remember, there are no harmful animals or predators in New Zealand and camping in the bush is safe. The only annoyances are the sandflies and the occasional mosquito so insect repellent should be carried.

As spring, summer, autumn (fall) and winter can all be experienced in one fishing day, it is wise to carry extra clothing and a reliable waterproof jacket.

In New Zealand very little fly fishing is done from boats or float tubes although both can be very useful at times. The extra weight and baggage handling is not worth the effort, however.

Access to most rivers and lakes is comparatively easy and the Queen's Chain exists on most waterways. The Queen's Chain is a legal right for the public to walk river banks and lake frontages provided there is public access to that river or lake. If there is no public access then permission must be obtained from the landowner. This is seldom denied unless farming operations such as lambing are under way.

We have carefully detailed some of the differences in fishing New Zealand waters. Understanding these variations will add to your enjoyment of this magnificent fishery.

CONSERVATION

New Zealand anglers are indeed privileged. We have some of the highest quality angling for wild trout anywhere in the world. However, there is no room for complacency.

In recent seasons, fish and game councils have sensibly reduced the bag limit in most districts. Overseas anglers have led the way with regard to catch and release and most Kiwi anglers are now practising such conservation measures. Briefly this involves:

- The use of the strongest practical nylon tippets to facilitate quick landing of fish. Long playing leads to the build-up of harmful metabolites such as lactic acid which kills fish even after they appear to swim away unscathed.

- Care in handling fish. Use a wide-mouthed net to minimise handling or release the fish while still in the water. Wet the hands first, avoid the gill area, do not squeeze the stomach and take care not to rub off scales. Turning the fish upside-down will often prevent it from struggling.

- The use of artery forceps or slim-jawed pliers for removing hooks.

- The use of barbless hooks. These can be difficult to obtain but ordinary hooks can easily be adapted by carefully crimping down the barb with slim-jawed pliers.

- Return the fish as quickly as possible. Some photographers keep fish out of the water far too long, considerably reducing their chances of recovery.

Anglers can assist fish and game councils and the Department of Conservation (DOC) by weighing and measuring all trout taken and supplying details from their diaries at the end of each season. This is especially important for fish that have been marked or tagged. Some landing nets now have scales in the handle to minimise the handling of fish. Tags should be returned along with the measurements to DOC. Metal or plastic tags are usually attached to the dorsal fin and fish can also be marked by fin clipping or even fin removal. To determine the right side of the fish from the left, look down on the fish's back with the head facing away from you. Always measure the fish from the fork of the tail to the tip of the snout. Send details of species, weight, length and time and area of capture. Angler cooperation is vital in managing a fishery.

Anglers should always extend courtesy to landowners. Few farmers will deny access to fishing water provided permission is sought first. Please shut gates, avoid disturbing stock and offer thanks on the way out. Remember, the cost of fishing in many other countries is well out of reach for most anglers. Fortunately, we have not yet reached that stage in New Zealand, but we must treat landowners with respect so access for others will not be denied. Most anglers we have met really care for the environment, but some fail to remove their rubbish and light fires indiscriminately. Should you decide to keep a fish for eating it should be cleaned well away from the river or lake edge, and fish guts must be deeply buried and not discarded into the waterway.

USEFUL INFORMATION

REGIONAL FISH AND GAME COUNCILS

North Island
Eastern: Box 1098, Rotorua, phone 07 348 0368
Tongariro/Taupo: Conservancy, Private Bag, Turangi,
    phone 07 386 8607
Wellington (Wairarapa): Box 1325, Palmerston North,
    phone 06 359 0409

South Island
Nelson/Marlborough: Box 2173, Stoke, phone 03 544 6382
West Coast: Box 179, Hokitika, phone 03 755 8546
Central South Island: Box 150, Temuka, phone 03 615 8400
Otago: Box 76, Dunedin, phone 03 477 9076
Southland: Box 159, Invercargill, phone 03 214 4501

WEATHER FORECAST (99 cents per minute)
Met Phone 0900 999 + Area Code
09 Auckland   04 Wellington (Wairarapa)
07 Bay of Plenty (Rotorua)   03 South Island

THE INTERISLANDER (Cook Strait passenger/car ferry service)
Call free 0800 802 802

CAR, FOUR-WHEEL-DRIVE AND MOTORHOME HIRE
Most major companies represented

METRIC CONVERSION TO US EQUIVALENTS (touring)
1 kilometre (km) = 0.6214 miles (m), that is km x 0.6 = miles
1 litre (l) = 0.2642 gallon (gal)

WEIGHTS AND MEASURES (weighing and measuring trout)

Metric measures and equivalents	*US measures and equivalents*
1 centimetre (cm) = 0.3937 in	1 inch (in) = 2.54 cm
1 kilogram (kg) = 2.2 lb	1 pound (lb) = 0.4536 kg

TEMPERATURES
Celsius to Fahrenheit: Multiply by $\frac{9}{5}$ then add 32
Fahrenheit to Celsius: Subtract 32 then multiply by $\frac{5}{9}$

Celsius	*Fahrenheit*	*Celsius*	*Fahrenheit*
0	32	40	104
5	41	45	113
10	50	50	122
15	59	60	140
20	68	80	176
25	77	100	212
30	86	120	248
35	95		

VISITOR INFORMATION NETWORK
Visitor information centres provide comprehensive local
information including:

■ bookings for accommodation

■ transport information and booking

■ itinerary planning and advice

■ sightseeing information and local attractions

- restaurant recommendations
- gifts and souvenirs
- stamps and phone cards

North Island

Auckland: Auckland Visitor Centre, PO Box 7048, Auckland
Phone 09 366 6888, fax 09 358 4684

Rotorua: Tourism Rotorua, Private Bag, Rotorua
Phone 07 348 5179, fax 07 348 6044

Taupo: Information Taupo, PO Box 865, Taupo
Phone 07 378 9000, fax 07 378 9003

Turangi: Turangi Information Centre, PO Box 34, Turangi
Phone 07 386 8999, fax 07 386 0074

Wellington: Visitor Information Centre, PO Box 2199,
    Wellington
Phone 04 801 4000, fax 04 801 3030

South Island

Christchurch: Canterbury Visitor Centre, PO Box 2600,
    Christchurch
Phone 03 379 9629, fax 03 377 2424

Dunedin: Dunedin Visitor Centre, PO Box 5457, Dunedin
Phone 03 474 3300, fax 03 474 3311

Gore: Gore Information Centre, PO Box 1, Gore
Phone 03 208 9908, fax 03 208 9908

Hokitika: Westland Information Centre, Private Bag,
    Hokitika
Phone 03 755 8322, fax 03 755 8026

Nelson: Nelson Visitor Information Centre, PO Box 194,
    Nelson
Phone 03 548 2304, fax 03 546 9008

Other local information centres are listed under each district.

NZ Professional Fishing Guides Association membership

Name	Street address	Town/City	Phone /Fax
Anthony Allan	65 Ocean View Terrace	Christchurch	03 326 5611 03 384 1477
Bill Allison	211 West Belt	Rangiora	03 313 8007 03 313 8007
Doug Andrew	21 Hallewell Road	Twizel	03 435 0729
Brent Beadle	Moana Motel, Ahau St	Westland	03 738 0083
Dean Bell	PO Box 198	Te Anau	03 249 7847 03 217 3755
John Boyles	RD 1 Blackball	Greymouth	03 732 3531
Brian Burgess	6 Mitre Street	Gore	03 208 0801
Ron Burgin	PO Box 1488	Taupo	07 378 3126 07 378 3126
Graeme Burnwin	Motupiko RD	Nelson	03 522 4052
John Burnwin	97 Murphy Street	Nelson	03 548 9145
Steven Carey	143 McKenzie Drive	Twizel	03 435 0300
Peter Carty	Chalgrave Street	Murchison	03 523 9525
Peter Church	13 Rangiamohia Road	Turangi	07 386 8621
Paddy Clark	Poronui Forest, RD 3	Taupo	07 384 2598
Ash Clement	Chatton RD 3	Gore	03 208 9446
Bryan Coleman	32 Kiwi Street	Rotorua	07 348 7766 07 347 9852
Bruce Collie	2 Rimu Lane	Wanaka	03 443 7236
Roy Coulson	6 Ingle Avenue	Taupo	07 378 7930 07 378 7930
Steve Couper	PO Box 149	Wakatipu	03 442 3589 03 442 3589
Boris Crech	Kehu Guiding, Rotoiti RD 2	Nelson	03 521 1840 03 521 1840
Trevor Cruikshank	Talbot Street 1 RD	Gore	
Peter Cullen	15 North Terrace	Gore	03 208 5677

Name	Street address	Town/City	Phone /Fax
Barry Davies	c/- Ormond Store, Ormond	Gisborne	
Graham Dean	c/- The Store, Te Rangiita	Turangi	
Simon Dickie	PO Box 682	Taupo	07 378 9680
David Dods	PO Box 38, Patutahi	Gisborne	06 862 7850
Ken Drummond	PO Box 186	Turangi	
Tony Entwistle	PO Box 88	Nelson	03 544 4565
Peter Flintoft	Owen River, PO Box 99	Murchison	03 523 9315
Dick Fraser	PO Box 145	Queenstown	03 442 6069
Kevin Frazier	104 Elizabeth Street	Ashburton	03 308 5963 03 308 1353
Jim Gosman	40 Herekiekie Street	Turangi	07 386 8996
Paul Greaves	PO Box 1976	Rotorua	07 348 1379
Lindsay Greenfield	Kilwell Sports, Private Bag, Rotorua		07 345 9094 07 345 5149
Clark Gregor	33 Haumoana Street	Rotorua	07 347 1123 07 347 1732
Arthur Grey	39 Matai Street	Wanaka	03 443 7279
Richard Halkett	Morris Lane	Pleasant Point	
John Hannabus	23 Milton Street	Gore	03 208 4922 03 208 9252
V Harvey	PO Box 52	Haast	03 750 0820
Tony Haynes	PO Box 278	Turangi	07 386 7946 07 386 8860
David Heine	111 Shakespeare Street	Greymouth	03 768 6415
Simon Hustler	PO Box 2	Gisborne	06 862 4809 06 862 4877
Fred Inder	132 Te Anau Terrace	Te Anau	
Basil Ivey	Cairn Hollow 5 RD	Ashburton	03 303 6078
Shane Johnston	20 Powell Crescent	Christchurch	03 358 6223
Chris Jolly	PO Box 1020	Taupo	07 378 0623

Name	Street address	Town/City	Phone /Fax
Jeff Jones	PO Box 624	Queenstown	03 442 6570
			03 441 8808
Bill Kirk	*NZ Fisherman,*		
	Private Bag, Parnell	Auckland	
Lloyd Knowles	Earnscleugh Road, RD 1	Alexandra	03 449 2122
Murray Knowles	PO Box 84	Te Anau	03 249 7565
			03 249 8004
Ron Mackay	PO Box 16, Owen River	RD 3 Murchison	03 523 9533
Harvey Maguire	Littles Road No 1 RD	Queenstown	03 442 7061
			03 442 7061
Ross Marks	12 Roa Road, Fendalton	Christchurch 4	03 348 2414
			03 379 0988
Dick Marquand	PO Box 32	Cromwell	
Graeme Marshall	Ngatimoti RD 1	Motueka	03 526 8800
Graeme Mathieson	6 Cleddau Street	Te Anau	03 249 7149
			03 249 7149
Tim McCarthy	PO Box 89	Turangi	07 386 8207
Bruce McClelland	38 Carters Terrace	Ashburton	03 308 7407
Hamish McCostie	35b Kawarau Place	Queenstown	
Geoff MacDonald	PO Box 443	Queenstown	03 442 8706
			03 442 8706
Brian Minty	17 Awamoa Road	Oamaru	03 434 7105
Mike Molineaux	Longridge Farm, RD 1	Te Anau	03 249 8070
George Moore	Unit 2, 34 Dublin St	Queenstown	03 442 5230
			03 442 5326
Zane Murfin	Baxter Street PDC	St Arnaud	03 521 1017
Frank Murphy	PO Box 16	Motu	06 863 5822
			06 863 5822
Tony Murphy	PO Box 1211	Queenstown	03 438 97 85
Scott Murray	174 Westbrook Terrace	Nelson	03 548 7826
David Murray-Orr	O'Grady Road, RD 1	Gisborne	06 868 6162
Martin J Noakes	63 Gillies Avenue	Taupo	07 378 4449
			07 378 4449

Name	Street address	Town/City	Phone /Fax
Rick Pollock	62 Arawa Road	Whakatane	07 308 5442
			07 307 1242
Eric Prattley	Wallingford Road	Temuka	03 615 9386
Len Prentice	50 Chensy Street	Invercargill	03 216 4447
Graham Pyatt	48 Rangipoia Place	Turangi	07 386 6032
Andrew Reid	PO Box 349	Turangi	07 386 0572
Stephen Saunders	5 McKinnon Loop	Te Anau	03 249 8364
			03 249 8674
Frank Schlosser	PO Box 124	Omarama	03 438 9408
Geoff Scott	The Cedars, RD 14	Rakaia	03 302 7444
			03 302 7220
Alan Simmons	48 Gosling Street	Turangi	07 386 7576
Glen Skinner	6 Johns Road	Rotorua	07 347 2363
			07 348 4069
Mike Stent	55 Lakewood Drive	Taupo	07 378 4449
Ron Stewart	Kiwistyle Safaris Ltd,		03 442 9966
	c/- Postal Centre	Glenorchy	03 442 9966
Gregory Sweetman	242 Kamo Road	Whangarei	09 437 7337
Harvey Taylor	34 Greenhurst Street	Christchurch	03 348 1971
Kevin Taylor	Sycamore Avenue,		03 302 1841
	RD 12	Barrhill	03 302 1841
Gerald Telford	210 Brownston Street	Wanaka	03 443 9257
			03 443 9257
Ronald Todd	PO Box 204	Te Anau	03 249 8187
Paul Van De Loo	Kikiwa Lodge RD 2	Nelson	
Peter Warren	Pigeon Valley Rd 2 RD	Wakefield	03 541 8500
			03 541 8500
Ray Watts	92 Michael Street	Rakaia	
Lindsay White	PO Box 68	Murchison	03 523 9114
			03 523 9114
Graham Whyman	c/- Sporting Life		
	Town Centre	Turangi	07 386 8996
Alan Wilson	411 Herbert Street	Invercargill	03 217 8687

GUIDE'S LICENCE

Fishing guides in New Zealand are now required by law to be registered. This legislation was actively supported by the professional guides in the industry as a·means of ensuring an adequate standard is maintained.

The legislation is controlled by the NZ Fish and Game Council and the criteria for a guide established in consultation with the industry. Licensed guides are for the client's protection, to ensure a professional and knowledgable guide.

FLY FISHING EQUIPMENT

LICENCE

To fish the North and South Islands of New Zealand two licences are required.

(1) New Zealand Licence — excludes Taupo region

(2) Taupo Licence — not effective in other regions of New Zealand

At present, both licences cost around $NZ60.00. A one-month comprehensive tourist licence for all New Zealand is also available. Contact: Tourism Rotorua, Private Bag, Rotorua, phone 07 348 5179

FOR SMALL AND MEDIUM-SIZED RIVERS

Fly rod: 4–6 weight	Reels (extra spools)
Floating line (preferably	Sink tip line
dark in colour)	Tippet: 3–6 lb
Leaders: 10–14 feet tapered	Forceps
Clippers	Net (optional)
Fly float	Scales
Indicator material	Hat
Fishing vest	Rain jacket
Polaroids	Camera and film
Wading boots	Water bottle
Wool socks	Thermos
Neoprene socks (optional)	Day pack

Flies

Caddis, mayflies and stoneflies are the main source of trout food. During the summer months brown and green manuka beetles, cicadas and hoppers play a major role in the food chain. We suggest the following assortment of flies but understand there will be personal preferences. A wide variety of flies will take fish.

Nymphs

Sizes 8–16
Beadheads (a wide selection)
Pheasant Tails
Hare and Copper (Hare's Ear)
Stoneflies (green, black and brown)

Dry flies

Sizes 10–16

Adams (parachute favoured)	Humpy
Royal Wulff	Hoppers
Stimulators	Irresistible
Twilight Beauty	Dad's Favourite
Elk Hair Caddis	Coch-y-bondhu
Green Beetle	Black Gnat

A small selection of emerger patterns, soft hackle wets, and well-weighted Woolly Buggers would also be advisable.

FOR LARGE RIVERS (I.E. TONGARIRO), LAKES AND STREAMS MOUTHS

Fly rod: 7–9 weight
Reels (extra spools)
Lines: floating, medium sink and shooting heads
Leaders: 9–12 feet tapered
Tippets: 5–10 lb
Waders: neoprene

Lures

(1) Stream mouth and lake fishing
    Rabbit flies (yellow and orange)
    Smelt patterns: Grey Ghost, Parson's Glory, Doll Fly

(2) For run fish
    Orange Rabbit
    Red Setter

(3) Night fishing
    Hairy Dog
    Fuzzywuzzy
    Craig's Night-time
    Black Marabou (with or without Aurora skirt)

(4) Nymph fishing for run fish
    Hare and Copper (well weighted)
    Flash Back
    Glow Bug
    Muppets
    Bug Eye

Please note: in the Taupo and Rotorua districts, no lead may be incorporated in the body of any fly larger than a number 10. Split shot, cork or polystyrene indicators are illegal; only synthetic or natural yarn may be used.

SUGGESTED ITINERARIES

Planning an itinerary is challenging as the options are limitless. Generally, the South Island offers better summer dry fly and nymph fishing to sighted fish in clear rivers, whereas the North Island has better lake, lure (wet fly), night and winter fishing. However, by following our guide, an angler could happily spend three or four weeks in summer in the North Island fishing some excellent water with a dry fly, nymph and lure. Anglers wishing to combine a winter skiing holiday in New Zealand should spend most of their time fishing in the North Island.

In summer, the South Island has so much water to fish that an angler could spend three weeks in one location and still not cover all the rivers, lakes and streams. If anglers wish to fish the South Island then they should plan to be there between the beginning of November and the end of March

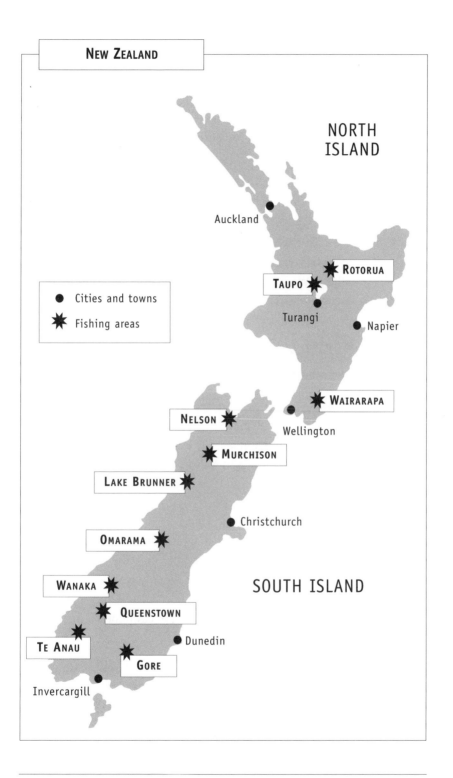

NEW ZEALAND

NORTH
ISLAND

Auckland

Cities and towns

Fishing areas

ROTORUA

TAUPO

Turangi

Napier

WAIRARAPA

NELSON

Wellington

MURCHISON

LAKE BRUNNER

Christchurch

OMARAMA

SOUTH ISLAND

WANAKA

QUEENSTOWN

TE ANAU

Dunedin

GORE

Invercargill

whereas good fishing is possible in the North Island throughout most of the year.

These facts should be borne in mind when planning an itinerary. For anglers wishing to catch a trophy rainbow, then lakes Aniwhenua, Rotoiti, Tarawera, Otamangakau and Okataina, and the Rangitikei River (all in the North Island), should be the venue. For anglers wanting a trophy brown trout then the more remote South Island backcountry is the preferred location.

NOTE: Our suggested itineraries provide only a guideline enabling you to select where you want to fish and spend your holiday. We recognise that weather and other unforeseeable circumstances may well dictate.

NORTH ISLAND

TWO OR THREE WEEKS IN WINTER (APRIL–JULY)

Note: neoprene waders and warm gear required.

Arrive Auckland and travel to Rotorua.

Arrange a professional guide and fish lakes Rotorua, Rotoiti, Tarawera, Okataina and Aniwhenua. Also the Rangitaiki and Horomanga rivers, and Wheao Canal. Suggest spending one week in the Rotorua area.

For the second week, travel to Taupo and Turangi and again seek the assistance of a professional guide. Fish some Taupo stream mouths at night, and the Tongariro and Tauranga-Taupo rivers during the day with nymph or lure. Visit Lake Otamangakau especially in April.

TWO OR THREE WEEKS IN SUMMER (NOVEMBER–MARCH)

Arrive Auckland and travel to Rotorua. Suggest fishing the Rangitaiki and Ruakituri rivers and Lake Rotorua stream mouths (three or four days).

Travel to Taupo. Try lakeshore smelt fishing to cruising rainbow, and stream mouth lure fishing both day and night.

Consider visiting the Rangitikei, Ngaruroro or Mohaka rivers by fixed wing or helicopter for sighted dry fly and nymph fishing. Lake Otamangakau is worth visiting for trophy fish. A float tube or boat is an advantage on this lake.

Travel to the Wairarapa and dry fly and nymph fish the Upper Manawatu, Makuri and Mangatainoka rivers (four or five days).

SOUTH ISLAND

TWO OR THREE WEEKS IN SUMMER (NOVEMBER–MARCH)

Arrive in Auckland and fly to Christchurch. Hire a car or camper.

Travel to Omarama, hire a professional guide and dry fly and nymph fish the rivers in this area according to the weather. This should include the Ahuriri, Hakataramea, Twizel and Tekapo rivers and Lake Benmore. One could spend weeks in this area but we suggest five days.

Travel to Wanaka and fish lakes Wanaka and Hawea for cruising fish and the Hunter River. At night in high summer, try the Clutha River with a sedge (five days).

Travel to Te Anau and hire a professional guide. Again depending on weather, fish the Mararoa, Upukeroro, Oreti, Eglinton, Worsley and Clinton rivers. Ten days could be easily spent in this area as a trip to Milford Sound is highly recommended.

• As an alternative, we suggest flying into Nelson from Auckland, booking a professional guide and fishing the Nelson, Murchison and Lake Brunner districts. Three weeks would pass by very quickly in these areas.

• For itineraries lasting four weeks or longer both South Island suggestions could be combined with Gore and Queenstown also included.

• To fish both North and South Islands a four-week visit would be a minimum in our opinion.

4

ROTORUA DISTRICT

Rotorua City, with a population of 65 000, lies in the Bay of Plenty in the northeastern part of the North Island and is a three-hour drive from Auckland and the International Airport. Rotorua is a tourist's mecca and is world famous for its geothermal activity and Maori culture. The New Zealand Maori Arts and Crafts Institute is located here. Taupo, Tauranga, with its orchards and beaches, and Whakatane, with its big game fishing, are each only an hour's drive away. In the Rotorua district there are seventeen lakes, exotic and native forests, rivers and farmland. The tourist attractions and cultural activities are diversified and include exploding mud pools, erupting geysers, steam vents, farm shows, Maori crafts and cultural performances, bush walks and hot spas. Additionally, Rotorua has two excellent golf courses.

As overseas tourists flock to this region, accommodation is seldom a problem but bookings should be made well in advance. Holiday parks, hotels, motels, backpackers, bed and breakfasts, homestays and farmstays are all available. At Lake Aniwhenua basic lodging is also available. And along the Ruakituri Valley road some farmers rent out shearers' quarters to anglers.

On non-fishing days we recommend touring the New Zealand Maori Arts and Crafts Institute, attending a hangi feast and concert, viewing the Waimangu Volcanic Valley, Rainbow Springs Wildlife Sanctuary, Te Whakarewarewa Thermal Reserve and the Buried Village, enjoying a hot soak in the Polynesian Spa, and visiting the Waiotapu Thermal Wonderland and the Agrodome.

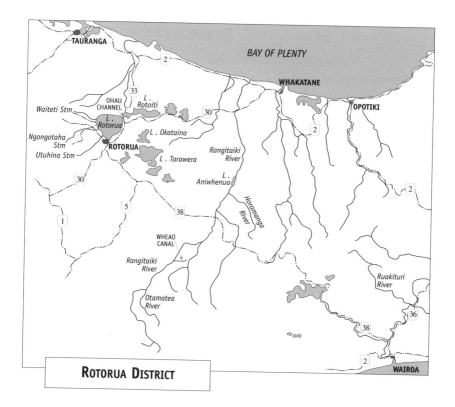

ROTORUA DISTRICT

For the hiker, a walk around Lake Tiki-Tapu (Blue Lake) or a stroll in the redwoods of the Whakarewarewa Forest can be most enjoyable. This area also offers a wide selection of attractive gardens and nurseries and the soil and climate produce magnificent rhododendrons, camellias and magnolias.

Rotorua's newly redeveloped city centre offers excellent shopping with easy parking and quality restaurants.

There are well-stocked fly shops in Rotorua and a number of professional trout fishing guides are available for hire.

More information can be obtained from:

Tourism Rotorua
Private Bag, Rotorua
Ph 07 348 4133
Fax 07 349 4133

Rotorua lakes and rivers

The Rotorua lakes offer wet fly and night fishing and are best fished in the autumn (fall), winter and spring months although stream mouth fishing in summer when the lakes are warm can also be rewarding. Likewise, trolling, harling (trolling with a fly rod) and jigging are productive methods of catching good-sized trout. Lakes Rotoiti, Okataina, Tarawera and Aniwhenua offer every chance of landing a trophy trout. The only river in this district within driving distance we would recommend is the Rangitaiki River. However, if heli-fishing is on the agenda, the Ruakituri River is well worth a fly-in.

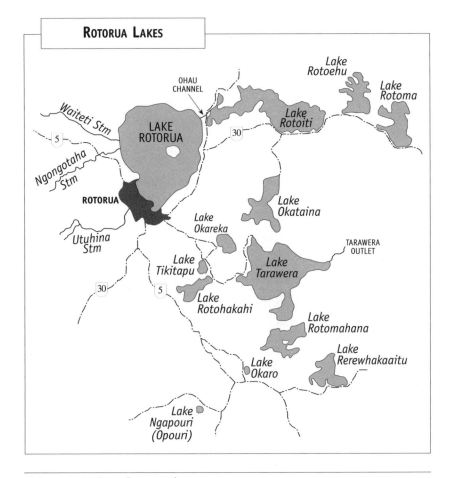

ROTORUA LAKES

LAKE ROTORUA

■ *Location and access*
Rotorua City lies on the southern shore and access is available all around the lake.

■ *Season*
Open season on the lake from 1 October to 30 September. For the streams flowing into the lake, 1 December to 30 June. Bag limit of eight trout.

■ *Boat launching*
Two ramps at Hamurana, two at Ngongotaha, two at Rotorua City, and one at Hannah's Bay. The ramps at the Soundshell, Motutara Point, Hannah's Bay, Hamurana, Ward Road (Hamurana), and Reeme Street (Ngongotaha) are concrete.

The lake covers 7878 ha and is relatively shallow, being 25 m deep in the deepest part. Apart from the built-up areas, the lake is surrounded by farmland. There have been pollution problems and in summer, blue-green algae have been troublesome. Water net and oxygen weed also grows prolifically in summer in the shallower bays. The shoreline is safe to   wade. Rainbows average 1–1.5 kg whereas brown trout average 3 kg.

Fly fishing from the shore
Stream mouths are favoured locations, especially after dark. When the lake temperature rises in summer, trout congregate in large numbers in the cooler, oxygenated water, and the fishing can be excellent from late December through to March. In April, trout begin their spawning runs and although fish can be taken, they do not congregate for any length of time before running. Stream mouths are all shallow so trout remain wary during the day unless the lake is ruffled by a stiff breeze. Fishing is best with an offshore breeze. Use a sink tip, floating or slow sinking line.

Recommended lures to use during the day are smelt patterns, Rabbit varieties, Dorothy, Hamill's Killer, Kilwell

No.1, Lord's Killer and Leslie's Lure. Some anglers fish a Glow Bug with success during the day. At night, use Craig's Night-time, Scotch Poacher, Fuzzywuzzy, Hairy Dog, Marabou patterns and Hamill's Killer. Luminous-bodied flies are favoured by some anglers including the Doll Fly.

Brown trout can also be stalked along the shore during the day. Try wading out some distance and look back into the shallows with Polaroid glasses. This type of fishing can be very exciting during January, February and March between Hamurana and the Ohau Channel. The cliffs help to eliminate water reflection thereby improving visibility. Large browns up to 4–5 kg can often be seen. Cast well ahead of cruising fish and use a small (size 8–10) smelt fly or even a nymph.

Spinning can be carried out from shore providing you are 300 m from any stream mouth. Fly casting at stream mouths is permitted from an anchored boat and can be most rewarding when the lake is warm.

Stream mouths

■ *Utuhina:* access from Arataua Street. There are some sunken logs and boulders at the mouth.

■ *Ngongotaha:* access from Beaumonts Road or Taui Street along the beach. Best when the wind is from the west.

■ *Waiteti:* from Arnold or Operina Street. Shallow mouth; wading is possible for 200 m from shore.

■ *Awahou:* access from Gloucester Street. Considered the most productive mouth and is heavily fished in January and February. Best in west or north-west winds.

■ *Hamurana Springs:* there is no fishing upstream of the road bridge. The mouth provides good fishing when the lake is warm as the Hamurana Stream is spring fed and cold.

Other small streams include the Waiowhiro, Waikuta, Waiohewa and the Waingaehe (Holdens Bay Stream). These will take only two or three rods and fish best with an offshore wind and floating line. Some need permission to reach through private property.

Trolling, jigging and harling
Half the trout caught in Lake Rotorua are landed from boats. Trolling, jigging and harling are prohibited within 300 m of stream mouths. The most difficult period for trolling is during January, February and March when fish gather in the cooler waters round stream mouths and water net fouls lures and outboard motors. Fish can be caught anywhere in the lake although round Mokoia Island is a favourite location. Other spots worth trying are off Kawaha Point, Sulphur Point, Hinemoa Point, the Airport Straight, Whakatane Turn-off and the Ohau Channel. Early morning or late afternoon are the most productive times. When harling a fly, use a high-density fly line (lead or wire lines are not permitted). The same flies recommended for stream mouths can be used for trolling, with the addition of Ginger Mick, Parson's Glory and Mrs Simpson.

When trolling a spinner try a black or green Cobra, Billy Hill, Tasmanian Devil, Black Toby or a Flatfish. Blue, black and green are favoured. Lake Rotorua can be treacherous in bad weather so keep an eye on the sky and wind.

ROTORUA STREAMS

■ *Utuhina:* crossed by SH 5 near Ohinemutu. The upper reaches above Pukehangi Road Bridge are closed to fishing.

■ *Ngongotaha:* access through private property off Valley Road.

■ *Waiteti:* the lower reaches can be reached from a footbridge near the mouth. The river is slow flowing and fishes better at night with a slow sinking line and black fly. Very popular with good fish taken during the cooler months. The upper reaches can be reached through private farmland north of Ngongotaha.

Only the Utuhina, Ngongotaha and Waiteti are open for fishing from 1 December to 30 June. In the early part of the season, recovering kelts can be taken on nymph and dry fly. However, the best fishing is later in the season, during April and May when run fish are in good condition. These can be taken on a small nymph or traditional lure but as the streams are small, often overgrown and clear, fishing is not easy.

OHAU CHANNEL
■ *Location and access*
Flows between Lake Rotorua and Lake Rotoiti. Much of the land bordering the channel is Maori held and permission should be sought. The Ohau Channel Camp proprietor will allow access to the camp area, except on opening day when only anglers staying at the camp have permission.

■ *Season*
1 October to 30 June. Bag limit of eight trout. Fishing is not permitted from an anchored boat within 100 m of the entrance or exit, nor is spin fishing allowed in the channel.

Fish live and spawn in the channel and also migrate through at certain times of the year. The water is deep, and a fast sinking line should be used. As there are few spawning areas in Rotoiti, many trout from this lake move through the channel to spawn in the Rotorua streams. For this reason, fishing tends to be good both early and late in the season — October to November and April to June are prime months.

During the day, try smelt patterns including Hawk and Silver, Silver Dorothy, Yellow and Silver Rabbit, Ginger Mick and Jack's Sprat. At night use the usual patterns especially Craig's Night-time, Scotch Poacher and 'lumo' flies.

THE DELTA
■ *Location and access*
This is the exit or mouth of the Ohau Channel into Lake Rotoiti. Access from SH 33 at the rest area 1.5 km east of Mourea.

Wading can be tricky as the bottom is uneven. The lip is also deep and drops off suddenly. Stand back 10 m or so from the lip and fish over it using a sinking line and a slow retrieve. April, May and June are the best months. Few anglers fish here at night, although there is no reason for this except perhaps the difficulties in wading. Use the same flies as for the channel with the addition of Hamill's Killer, Kilwell No.1 and Mrs Simpson.

LAKE ROTOITI

■ *Location and access*
East of Lake Rotorua connected by the Ohau Channel. SH 30 follows the southern shoreline and SH 33 the western shoreline.

■ *Season*
1 October to 30 June. For shoreline anglers only from Ruato Bay to Hineopu, and the Kaituna River below Okere, 1 July to 30 September. Bag limit of eight trout. No lead or wire lines.

■ *Boat launching*
Otaramarae, Waipuna Bay, Gisborne Point and Hinehopu. All are concrete or bitumen except Waipuna which is pumice. Otaramarae is the deepest.
Rotoiti is the third largest lake in the Rotorua area and covers 3340 ha. The northern shore is bushclad.

Fly fishing
Over the last few years, 'r' type late-maturing rainbow fry have been regularly released from the shore between Ruato Bay and Hinehopu. When mature, these fish return to their release site to spawn. As a result, fly fishing has dramatically improved with fish over 4.5 kg not uncommon. The best fishing is from April to the end of October.

Use a floating, sink tip, or slow sinking line and during the day try Red Setter, Parson's Glory, Kilwell, Hamill's Killer, Mrs Simpson or Jack's Sprat. Some anglers have success with Glow Bugs and Muppets. At night, try Hairy Dog, Scotch

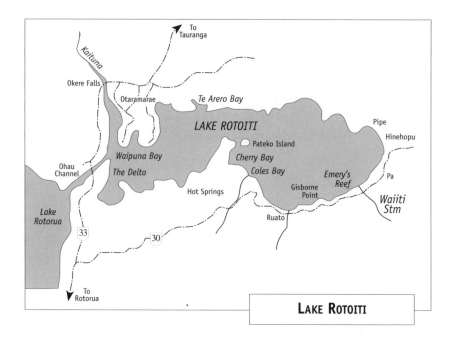

Poacher, Taihape Tickler, Black Phantom or Craig's Night-time. Luminous body flies are very popular, especially Doll Fly and Black Phantom. Many anglers use two flies at night.

Most fish are in shallow water close to shore, so false casting and quiet fishing with a slow retrieve is essential. Fish we have caught are often full of very large smelt.

When fishing Rotoiti it is wise to have at least 100 m of backing on your reel as although some fish are disappointing fighters, others just never stop.

The following shoreline spots are recommended.

■ *Haupara Bay:* This is the first bay reached from Rotorua. Access down a driveway opposite the bus stop. A small stream mouth can be located 30 m down the beach to your right. This bay closes on 30 June as wild fish spawn in this stream.

■ *Ruato (Twin Stream) Bay:* SH 30 runs the length of this popular bay and the odd logging truck has been caught on the back cast. The two streams empty into the lake at either end of the sandy beach, but the larger stream at the right-hand end provides the best fishing. An offshore wind is desirable and fish can be caught off the beach using a floating line. Start at dusk and if the fishing is slow until 9.30 pm it is probably not worth persisting. If the fishing is poor at Ruato then it may be better at Hinehopu.

■ *Emery's Reef:* This spot is opposite Emery's Store. Enter the lake on the right side of the jetty and wade quietly along the shore for 80 m to a large karaka tree on the bank above. There is an old engine block to stand on. The reef can be covered by casting slightly to your left. A cold spring near the reef attracts fish.

■ *Gisborne Point:* This can be reached by wading further along the shore from Emery's Reef. There is another cold spring here close to the shore.

■ *Waiiti Stream:* SH 30 crosses this stream. Access to the mouth is from the eastern side of the bridge. Fishes best in windy conditions, especially a northerly. Will hold four or five rods.

■ *Quarry (dump):* The quarry and rubbish collection area is easily seen from SH 30 and access is easy from the road to the lake. The lake shore fishes well in a westerly all along this shoreline, from the quarry past the 'Transformer' and the 'Pipe' to the Bluff at Hinehopu. There is good safe wading.

■ *The Pipe:* lies at the far end of the beach past the baches at Hinehopu. At the pipe wading should be avoided and a slow or medium sinking line used. Fishes best after heavy rain when water flows through the pipe from the swamp behind. There is good fishing beyond the Pipe to the bush-covered bluff but wading is required here to avoid the bush on the backcast. Watch for old, slippery, sunken logs along the sandy beach.

Trolling, jigging and harling

A lot of fish are caught trolling, jigging and harling from a boat. Recommended areas include the northern bushclad shore, Sulphur Bay, Pateko Island, Cherry Bay, Coles Bay and Te Arero Bay. Harling a fly on a high-density fly line is often more effective than trolling hardware. Some anglers use graphite-coated lines (lead) in order to sink their lure. Try Parson's Glory, Orange Rabbit, Red Setter, Tassies, Cobras, Billy Hill, Pearl or a Toby. Black and red are popular colours.

Two of our bridge-playing companions have had some success off the bushclad shore near Hinehopu. Their technique is to tie their boat to an overhanging tree, cast a spinner out over the blue line, read the Sunday paper and then slowly retrieve.

Trout will also respond to ledgering a Glow Bug but this method is not for the purist. Fish take the lure well down and it becomes impossible to release fish without trauma.

LAKE TARAWERA

■ *Location and access*

Lies southeast of Rotorua. Turn right off the Whakatane Highway at Ngapuna and drive 15 km, past the Buried Village. The outlet can be reached through the Tasman forestry from Kawerau (a permit is required from the forestry manager).

■ *Season*

1 October to 30 June except for the Main Beach (Landing) and the Orchard, which have an open season for fly fishing only. The outlet is permanently closed but fishing is permitted 150 m downstream of the outlet to the falls from 1 October to 31 May. Wire and lead lines can be used but no trolling is permitted within 300 m of any stream mouth nor within the confines of Rangiuru Bay. All other streams are closed to fishing. Bag limit of eight trout.

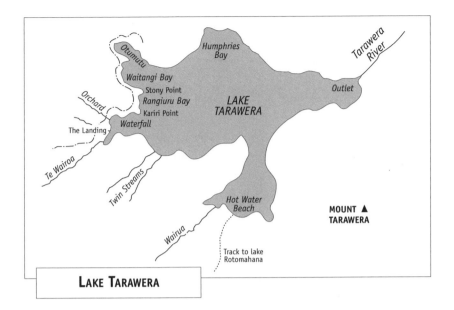

LAKE TARAWERA

■ *Boat launching*
Concrete ramps at the Main Beach (Landing) and Stony Point Reserve, and pumice launching areas at Kariri Point boatsheds, Raniuru Bay, Otumutu and Te Tapahoro.

Tarawera has always been a dark, forbidding lake to us. It is very deep and dominated by the dormant volcano Mount Tarawera. Bushclad hills surround most of the shoreline and in winter, Tarawera can be cold and inhospitable. The lake can come up very rough during a strong southerly or even in an easterly — boat owners be warned. The lake has been renowned in the past for its wild trophy rainbow up to 7 kg in weight. Since 1985, fish size has diminished and it is now exceptional to catch a fish over 5 kg. It is thought exotic forest plantings have altered the nitrogen-phosphate ratio in the lake water, resulting in blooms of blue-green algae. This affects the zooplankton which provide food for smelt, the principal trout food. Despite this, some excellent fish can be caught in this lake.

Shoreline fishing

Stream mouths are the top spots during April, May and June, but angling pressure can be intense. Some fish can be taken in the daytime, but most are caught in the evening, early morning and at night. Legal fishing time is from 5 am to midnight irrespective of daylight saving. At the Te Wairoa Stream mouth, we have been fourth in line at 4.15 am waiting to enter the water at 5 am.

Favoured lures include Kilwell No.1, Red Setter, Hamill's Killer, Leslie's Lure, Green Smelt, and Parson's Glory, in sizes 6–8, while at night the usual night fly patterns are effective as well as the luminous Doll Fly.

The following are favoured spots.

■ *The Wairoa Stream mouth:* Follow the track to the right from the car park at the Landing for 150 m. Holds five or six rods but care is needed when wading as the drop-off is very deep. Stand back and fish quietly over the lip. At night use a slow or medium sinking line and during the day use a fast sinker or shooting head. There is a weed bank to the right of the mouth and at night fish can be taken on a floating line over this bank. Fishes best in a westerly or southwesterly.

As a conservation measure for wild 'r'-type rainbow, all jack fish caught within a radius of 200 m of this stream mouth must be released unharmed. This becomes a problem for anglers fishing with Glow Bugs. With this 'heave and leave' method, trout tend to take these lures well down into their gullet and releasing fish unharmed is impossible.

■ *The Main Beach (Landing):* Turn off the main Tarawera road onto Spencer Road. During an easterly, anglers crowd this beach as schools of fish move close into the stirred-up waves. Even if one is not fishing, the action can be quite amazing at times.

Many of the fish taken will be foul hooked and must be released. Use a slow sinking line and a Red Setter or Killer pattern during the day; at night the same as for Te Wairoa Stream.

- *The jetties:* Use a sinking line off the jetties but a floater if fishing the tiny stream mouth to the left of the jetty. Best at night. Fishes best in a westerly or southwesterly.

- *The Orchard:* Walk to the left from the car park beneath the rocky bluff to a small stream which empties into shallow water. Only holds two rods and false air casting with a floating line is recommended. Start well back as fish move close in during early morning and at dusk. Fishes best in a westerly or southwesterly.

- *Rangiuru Bay:* Drive past Spencer Road to Rangiuru Road. This leads to a picnic area and boat ramp by the willows. This bay is closed to trolling. Wading is necessary and the most popular spot is in the southwest corner. There is a broad, sandy shelf out in front of a bush-covered promontory with acacia trees on the skyline. Fish can be taken during the day but night fishing provides the best sport. Use a luminous-bodied Doll Fly or a Black Phantom tied with the same body material — Aurora skirt. It pays to carry a landing net else a long walk back to shore is required to land a fish. Fishes best in a westerly or southwesterly.

- *Waitangi Bay:* Access to this spot is from the end of Waitangi Road. Follow a path to a foreshore reserve and round into the bay. Similar to the Orchard. Best in a light onshore wind and use a floating line at night with false casting.

- *The Waterfall:* Enters Te Wairoa Bay beyond the Orchard and can only be fished by casting from an anchored boat.

- *Twin Streams:* Access by boat between Te Wairoa and the Wairua Arm. Fly cast from an anchored boat or wade the shelf and fish over the lip.

- *Wairua Stream mouth:* Boat fishing is not permitted within 15 m of the stream mouth. Access is by boat to the head of the Wairua Arm. Very heavily fished in April, May and June but can offer great sport. It can also be frustrating especially during the day when the water literally turns pink from the great school of fish waiting off the stream mouth. Fishes better with two or three rods but that is a rare event these days. We have slept a number of nights curled up in a boat at this spot only to be kept awake after midnight by trout splashing their way up the stream.

Trolling, jigging and harling
This can be very slow in the hot summer months and most fish are caught on lead or wire lines just off the blue line or shelf. Harling a size 4 Parson's or Yellow Rabbit on a high-density line can be productive in October to November, especially in the early morning or evening. Favoured spinners include Flat Fish, Tasmanian Devil, Toby, Cobra and the Zed Spinner. Fish can be taken anywhere and at any time providing one has patience. It is a matter of finding the fish and fishing the right depth.

LAKE OKATAINA

■ *Location and access*
Turn right at Ruato on SH 30 and travel for 6 km along a scenic, bush-lined road to the lake.

■ *Season*
1 October to 30 June. Open season for fly fishing only from the main beach at Home Bay. Fishing is prohibited from a boat within 15 m of the Log Pool.

■ *Boat launching*
Ramp at Home (Tauranganui) Bay.

This beautiful, deep lake is surrounded by native bush. Since the introduction of 'r'-type late-maturing rainbow fry over the past few years, this lake, along with Lake Rotoiti, has become the trophy lake for the Rotorua district. Fish weighing over 6 kg have been caught by fly casting from the shore and fishing from a boat. You will need 100 m of backing on your reel. As with Lake Rotoiti, there are few spawning streams entering this lake so fish move into the shallows during the colder months in search of spawning beds.

When fly casting from the shore during the day use a slow or medium sinking line but at night use a floater. Wading is required and is safe. A wide variety of flies will take fish. These include Red Setter, Green Hairy Dog, Parson's Glory, Doll Fly, Mrs Simpson, smelt and Rabbit varieties, Glow Bug and Muppet. Fish can be taken anywhere along the shore with Rocky Point and the Log Pool being top locations.

If fly fishing from an anchored boat, use a high-density or shooting head line and fish deep over weed beds. Some anglers have success ledgering a Glow Bug but the flies listed above will all take fish. Prime spots are stream mouths, the Log Pool, Te Koutu (Maori) Point, Parimata and Kaiakahi Bays. As is usual in the Rotorua lakes, fish go deep during January, February and March.

In summer, the secret for success in trolling or harling this lake is to get down deep so lead or wire lines or a length of such a line attached to monofilament is necessary. Use the flies listed for fly casting and try spinners such as Toby, Flatfish, Cobra, Penny and Tasmanian Devil.

RANGITAIKI RIVER

This river rises on Lochinvar Station south of the Napier-Taupo Road and flows in a northerly direction through the Kaingaroa Forest and down through Murupara, Galatea, Matahina and Edgecumbe to enter the sea near Thornton. There are three hydro-electric dams on this river forming Flaxy Lake and lakes Aniwhenua and Matahina. In addition, above the Rangitaiki-Wheao confluence, the river has been diverted into the Rangitaiki-Wheao Canal. Only the upper section of this river in the Kaingaroa Forest is described here as the other sections are difficult, overgrown and less productive. A permit from Fletcher Challenge Forests at the Whakarewarewa Visitors Centre, PO Box 1748, Rotorua is required to enter Kaingaroa Forest and a map of the forestry roads should also be purchased as it is easy to get lost.

Rangitaiki River

■ *Location and access*
Turn off SH 38 into the Kaingaroa Forest on Wairapakau Road, then onto Low Level Road. Turn into Te Awa campsite which offers basic facilities and travel south on Eastern Boundary Road. This follows the true left bank as far as the Otamatea confluence. There is access from the Taupo-Napier Road (SH 5) but this can be confusing for first-time anglers.

There are 25 km of fishable water within the exotic forest and this stretch of river is highly regarded by anglers. However, this river is not easy to fish as the banks are lumpy, swampy and overgrown by toetoe, gorse and scrub. Casting can be frustrating. Drift dives reveal there are 98 medium-sized rainbow and a smaller number of browns per kilometre of river. The river bed is pumice, shingle, rock and weed and although the river is deep and slow flowing in most sections, there are a few rapids, pools and runs. Trout can be spotted close to the banks on calm, clear low water conditions but a lot of anglers fish the river blind. There is an active evening rise and fish will rise during the day in favourable weather conditions.

Useful flies include beadhead nymphs for the deeper stretches, Pheasant Tail and Hare's Ear nymphs, Parachute Adams, Dad's Favourite, Humpy, Royal Wulff, Coch-y-bondhu, Black Gnat and Elk Hair Caddis dry flies, and soft hackle wet flies.

The Otamatea tributary is overgrown and best fished by wading upstream from the confluence with the Rangitaiki. There are a few deep holes but fish can be spotted and stalked in clear water. There is only 2.5 km of river to fish.

RANGITAIKI-WHEAO CANAL

■ *Location and access*
This canal connects the Rangitaiki River to the Wheao hydro-electric scheme. There are good access roads to both sides of the canal which are signposted on Low Level Road.

■ *Season*
1 October to 30 June.

The canal is 20 m wide and 8 m deep in the middle, and casting is easy. Trout cannot easily be spotted, but there are good stocks of brown and rainbow up to 3 kg. There is an abundance of insect life and fish rise freely in favourable conditions. Use the same flies as listed for the Rangitaiki.

LAKE ANIWHENUA

■ *Location*
Lies north of Murupara and Galatea. Access to the top end of the lake from Rabbit Bridge and the causeway on Kopuriki Road; to the middle of the lake from Galatea Road across private land, and to the dam campsite and lower reaches from Black Road.

■ *Season*
Open season from 1 October to 30 September. Bag limit is two trout.

Formed in 1980, this hydro lake, covering 200 ha, averages

only 2.5 m in depth, except for some deep holes along the old Rangitaiki river bed. The eastern shoreline is farmland, while the western shore is scrub covered and unfishable from the shore. This lake has a reputation for wild, trophy fish and in 1993, six fish over 5 kg were caught. As the shoreline is difficult, a boat or float tube can be very useful to find some of the deep holes in the old river bed. Fish can be taken from the shore but are not easy to spot. In summer, oxygen and net weed can be a problem although since February 1996, net weed has mysteriously disappeared. This may be the reason for a decline in the size of fish caught recently as the net weed harboured large numbers of water worms which are a great food source for trout. Oxygen weed holds snails and trout also feed on these.

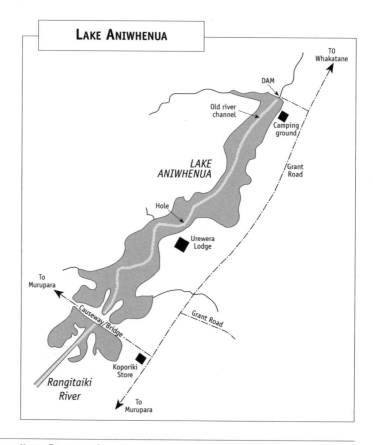

LAKE ANIWHENUA

TO Whakatane

DAM

Old river channel

Camping ground

LAKE ANIWHENUA

Grant Road

Hole

Urewera Lodge

To Murupara

Causeway Bridge

Grant Road

Koporiki Store

Rangitaiki River

To Murupara

Lake Aniwhenua

The lake fishes best in the cooler months of the year, especially April, May and June, but fish can be taken year round. Trolling, harling, jigging, spinning and fly casting can all be successful. For the fly angler we suggest trying small nymphs such as Hare's Ear and Beadhead Pheasant Tail; Beadhead Woolly Buggers, Damsel nymphs, Hamill's Killer, Red Setter and Black Marabou lures at night.

HOROMANGA RIVER

■ *Location*
Rises in the bushclad western hills of the Urewera National Park and joins the Rangitaiki River 3 km above Lake Aniwhenua. Access from Galatea.

■ *Season*
1 October to 30 June. Bag limit one trout. Fly fishing only.

The lower reaches are rather unstable having been used for shingle extraction. Plans are in place for this section of river to be improved as the Horomanga is a vital spawning stream for Lake Aniwhenua. Some large fish enter the river in April, May and June and fishing can also be good at the beginning of October. Fish can be spotted and stalked with small nymphs and Glow Bugs. This river holds small rainbow most of the year but the spawning run holds most of the attraction for anglers. There are good stable pools in the bush for active anglers prepared to walk. It is recommended that large fish caught be weighed, photographed and returned unharmed to the river.

RUAKITURI RIVER

■ *Location*
Although this river lies in the Eastern Fish and Game Council District, it is a very long and difficult drive from Rotorua. The river runs northeast of Lake Waikaremoana and if this lake is being visited, then an extra 90-minute drive to the Ruakituri Valley is recommended. It is an outstanding fishery; the cost of hiring a helicopter from Rotorua is worth investigating.

■ *Season*
1 October to 30 June. Fly fishing only. Above Waitangi Falls, bag limit is two trout; below the falls, eight trout.

This relatively inaccessible, medium-sized river provides superb fly fishing for over 30 km of main river. The stretch of water from Erepeti Bridge to Papuni Station would be hard to better in New Zealand, especially for the nymph angler. The river holds an excellent stock of rainbow and brown trout which average around 2 kg but fish are not easy to spot except in low-water summer conditions when browns occupy pocket water near the edges. Crossings are possible at the tail of some pools but the river bed is very slippery to wade. Fishing is possible through both the Erepeti and Papuni gorges in low water but Papuni Station claims riparian rights and discourages anglers. However, a personal approach is worthwhile, especially if one is prepared to

Ruakituri River

tramp for two to three hours from the end of Papuni Road to reach the Waitangi Falls. Above these falls are trophy rainbow up to 6 kg but they are not easy to catch. Some tramping and camping experience is required for such a visit. As this river runs through papa country it easily discolours after rain and takes 48 hours to clear. The river can be unfishable in the lower reaches but fishable higher up as side creeks from cleared farmland carry most of the silt.

Many flies will take fish but well-weighted nymphs, especially beadhead patterns and stoneflies, should be carried. An effective summer rig is a small beadhead Hare's Ear tied to the bend of the hook of a hopper pattern.

TAUPO DISTRICT

Lake Taupo, the largest lake in New Zealand, lies in the centre of the North Island and is a popular tourist destination. It is a three-and-a-half-hour drive from Auckland and a five-hour drive from Wellington. There are scheduled daily bus services from many North Island cities and towns and an hour flight from Auckland International Airport.

Taupo is a sophisticated quality venue with modern accommodation, good restaurants and shopping facilities. There are two excellent golf courses, natural thermal spas and a host of other scenic attractions including two natural thermal areas in close proximity, Wairakei Park and Orakei Korako. In addition, Honey Hive New Zealand, the Huka Falls, and the world's only geothermally heated prawn farm are all within a 30-minute drive from the town centre. Scenic lake cruises, bush walks and horse treks also create a diversion for non-fishing days.

Turangi, at the southern end of the lake, is a 40-minute drive from the Taupo township and invites one to try white water rafting, tramping and skiing in the Tongariro National Park and a hot soak in the thermal spa at Tokaanu. The Tongariro National Trout Centre (hatchery) just south of Turangi merits a visit and can be scheduled to coincide on a day when you will be fishing the Birch pools on the Tongariro River nearby.

There are well-stocked fly shops in both Taupo and Turangi and both centres have professional trout fishing guides available for hire.

For ease of reference, three wild and scenic rivers lying east of the Taupo district are described in this chapter; the Rangitikei, Ngaruroro and Mohaka rivers.

For more information:
Taupo District Council, Private Bag 2005, Taupo
Ph 07 377 9855, Fax 07 377 2029

Turangi Information Centre, PO Box 34, Turangi
Ph 07 386 8999, Fax 07 386 0074

TAUPO DISTRICT TROUT

Ova from European brown trout (*Salmo trutta*) were brought to the South Island from Tasmania in 1867 and to Taupo in 1886. Rainbow trout (*Salmo gairdnerii*) ova from Sonoma Creek in San Francisco Bay were obtained in 1883, hatched in a pond in the Auckland Domain and liberated in Lake Taupo in 1897. All the rainbow trout in New Zealand have originated from this one shipment. Food sources in this lake were plentiful and included the striped kopuku (a small native grayling), koura (freshwater crayfish), inanga (whitebait) and cockabully. Trout thrived and by 1910 fish weighing 9 kg were being caught. In the 1920s the food supply was being depleted to such a low level that fish lost condition and the Government introduced netting to reduce stocks. Then in 1934 a smelt (*Retropinna*) was introduced as a food source. This was very successful and now constitutes the main food supply for Taupo trout.

Between April and September, 60 percent of trout in Lake Taupo run up rivers and streams entering the lake to spawn. Spent fish (kelts or slabs) return to the lake at much the same time that smelt school into the shallows and river mouths to spawn, that is October–December. Fish feed voraciously to regain condition. Fry that have hatched and survived enter the lake nine to twelve months later as fingerlings 15–20 cm long. In two to four years, these fingerlings reach maturity, and so the cycle continues.

LAKE TAUPO

The lake, the largest in New Zealand, is 40 km long, 30 km wide and covers more than 600 sq km. It has an average depth of 120 m, the deepest point being 160 m, and lies at 360 m above sea level.

This fishery fully deserves its worldwide reputation, as it offers a wide variety of superb angling water. Over 1200 tonnes of trout are landed each year. The average weight of each fish caught is approximately 1.6 kg. Fish over 4 kg are not uncommon although most of these are brown trout. A friend recently witnessed an overseas visitor nonchalantly walking up the Tokaanu wharf carrying a rainbow weighing 6.8 kg landed while trolling.

The movement of trout in the lake follows the smelt life cycle. From October to January 'smelt fishing' can be had along the shoreline and at river mouths. From October to the end of May feeding fish can be caught at river mouths, but shoreline fishing is unproductive after January. From the end of May, when river water temperatures equal lake temperatures, fish feed in the deeper waters of the lake and only enter stream mouths briefly prior to running up to spawn. Deep trolling then becomes an effective method.

Fish can still be caught during the winter months, but action tends to be slower in the lake, whereas river fishing comes into its own.

Fly fishing at stream and river mouths

Trout feed along the lip where the river delta drops off into deeper water and along the edges of the current where it merges with the lake water. It is important to stand back a few metres from the lip as fish often take the fly during the retrieve as it passes over the lip. Wading is usually necessary, however, and waders are essential to protect against the cold water. In shallow mouths, thigh waders are adequate but chest waders are needed for deeper water.

False casting in the air is recommended at shallow

mouths as excessive water disturbance, even at night, frightens feeding fish. Most Taupo stream mouths can be fished with either a medium sinking or floating line, and a weight forward line will enable a longer cast to be made, an important factor when fishing pressure is high.

Generally, a strong onshore wind makes fishing difficult. When the current parallels the shore, the prime spot may be 50 m along the beach. However, a light onshore breeze may be conducive to good fishing.

■ *Season*

Open season on the lake and lower reaches of most rivers. Bag limit reduced to three fish from December 1990 due to depletion of fish stocks. Nymph size (any fly with lead incorporated in the body) now reduced to 10 hook (see licence for details), that is length 17 mm, gap 5.5 mm. No split shot, polystyrene or cork indicators may be used; only natural or synthetic yarn is allowed.

There is no substitute for experience as each stream mouth has its own characteristics. However, when the fishing is slow, a number of options may be tried. Try changing position but before doing so always ask other anglers and do not force your way into the prime spot unless there is an obvious gap or you are joining the end of the line. Sometimes, fish do not feed along the lip and it may be worth wading well out and casting into the tail of the current. Do not fish in front of another angler and if in doubt, check before making such a move.

Other tactics when the fishing is slow include changing lines, trying a smaller fly or changing fly patterns. Some flies do not swim well and even changing flies of a similar pattern can make a difference. Altering the speed of the retrieve may also bring success. Remember, your fly should swim to resemble a smelt or if fishing slowly and deeply, a koura (freshwater crayfish).

At very small stream mouths, fishing improves if the

current runs straight out into the lake. Wading may not be necessary at some small stream mouths and periodically resting such water for fifteen minutes can entice trout back into the shallows. It may be difficult to convince others to cooperate with this action.

Fishing is generally better on dark, moonless nights but do not be discouraged by other conditions as we well remember taking ten fish on a Red Setter when the moon was full and bright.

During the day when fish are smelting through the rip, action can be fast and furious or totally frustrating. Trout can be seen gorging on smelt and although many of these fish will be kelts, fishing is invariably fascinating. Try a very small smelt fly, even as small as a number 10 or 12. When all else fails a nymph fished along the edge of the current can bring surprising results.

■ *Flies during the day*
Green Smelt, Taupo Tiger, Split Partridge, Grey Ghost, Mallard Smelt, Hawk and Silver, Parson's Glory, Jack's Sprat, Doll flies or Ginger Mick in overcast conditions. Sizes 6–10 preferred. Just to confound the experts, we watched a friend take a limit on a Hairy Dog one bright sunny day.

■ *Flies for night*
Marabou flies, Hairy Dog, Fuzzywuzzy, Black Phantom, Scotch Poacher, Guardsman, Black Rabbit or Craig's Night-time in sizes 2–6. We prefer the larger sizes but a stronger trace is advised up to 5.5 kg. When all else fails at night, try a daytime smelt pattern or a luminous-bodied fly.

Smelt fishing along the beaches
Walking the beaches looking for smelting fish on a hot bright day is our favourite Taupo fishing. November and December are the prime months. Shorts, sandshoes, Polaroids, hat and sunscreen are essential items.

Schools of fish can be seen at times breaking the surface and throwing caution to the wind in their efforts to feed on

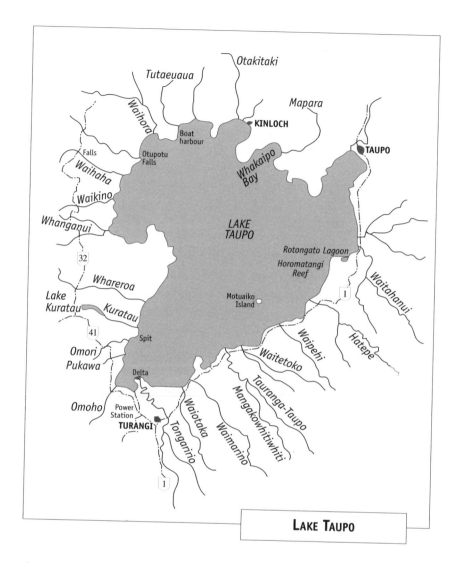

LAKE TAUPO

these tiny spawning fish. A quick cast and a fast retrieve is required using a floating line and a small smelt fly. In very calm conditions, casting at fish frightens them. A sinking line casts no shadow and if the fly is landed well away from cruising fish and retrieved as the trout approaches, a take can be anticipated. This is an exciting way to fish but requires patience.

Fishing the rivers

Trout run up the Taupo rivers from March to November, the heaviest runs occurring after a storm and heavy rain. By July, the rivers are full of fish and by September many fish will be spent and drifting back to the lake. Trout tend to lie in the deeper parts of pools or under banks where there is maximum cover. Each pool has a favoured lie, and some have more than one, but to be successful an angler must ensure that the lure or nymph being fished reaches a depth sufficient to entice a take. This means 'dredging' the bottom.

■ *Downstream lure*

In the smaller rivers, a light 2.5 m rod and a medium sinking line is all that is required. In the Tongariro, a 3 m rod and a high-density or shooting head line is advisable. A trace of 2–2.5 m is sufficient as a longer trace tends to allow the fly to float higher. Use a trace of 3.5–5 kg breaking strain in the larger rivers, lighter in the smaller streams. The lure should be cast across the river or even slightly upstream in a big pool, allowed to sink deeply as it drifts with the current, swung through the lie and retrieved.

The 'take' usually occurs at the end of the swing and there is nothing as exciting as a fresh-run rainbow of 2.5 kg smashing the fly. Mending the line to take up the slack is advised as the line begins to swing. Subtle variations can be made by altering the speed of the retrieve or letting out more line.

Favoured lures include Rabbit flies, Red Setter, Hairy Dog, Mrs Simpson, Dappled Dog, Mallard patterns, smelt varieties, and Leslie's Lure. Many new patterns are being produced, some with fluorescent bodies, but it is difficult to improve on the first two listed. Some anglers even fish a Glow Bug or Muppet in a similar fashion.

■ *Upstream nymph*

With the introduction of lightweight rod materials, the same-sized rods can be used for both methods of fishing. Use a weight forward number 8–10 floating line for the

Tongariro, and a lighter number 6–8 on the smaller streams. Naturally, the line weight should match the rod.

For the smaller streams one weighted nymph is sufficient but in the heavier water many anglers use two heavily weighted nymphs placed from twelve to 60 cm apart. The proximal nymph acts as a weight as most fish take the smaller distal nymph. The short trace attached to the distal nymph is tied to the eye of the hook of the proximal nymph. When fishing heavy water use a long trace up to 5 m in length, but be aware, casting can become very difficult with this rig, especially in a strong wind. Pulling up your parka hood may not primarily be to protect you from the weather!

A long cast upstream ensures your nymph has plenty of time to sink and drift through the lie, scraping the stones on the bottom. Allow the nymph to float down naturally with the current with no drag. It is important to keep the line as straight as possible so immediate contact with the fish can be made should a take occur. Most anglers use an indicator attached to the end of the flyline which could be a quill, a bunch of wool or synthetic yarn. When the indicator deviates in its downstream course, stops or sinks, an immediate strike must be made before the fish rejects the deception. Some anglers now run their trace through a Fuller's Earth and glycerine mixed to reduce surface tension on the nylon thereby allowing it to sink rapidly. Others use detergent or river sand for the same purpose.

All water can be explored with a nymph and it is surprising how fish choose to lie in pockets of very rough water. A wide variety of nymphs will take fish although the smaller sizes are more consistently accepted. For this reason, the proximal nymph is often large (long shank size 10) and heavily weighted while the distal nymph can be size 12 or even as small as size 14.

Favoured nymphs and deceptions include beadhead patterns, Hare and Copper, Bug Eye varieties, Half Back, White Caddis and Pheasant Tail nymphs, or egg imitations like Muppet and Glow Bug.

FAVOURED LOCATIONS

Trout can be caught anywhere in Lake Taupo. Stream mouths are top locations but many rocky points around the lake can also provide good fishing. Trout tend to cruise the 'blue line' or drop-off, the junction between inshore shallows and deeper water. Before selecting a spot to fish, make certain there is not a strong onshore wind.

STREAM AND RIVER MOUTHS

Eastern lake shore

■ *Mangakura Stream:* Enters the lake 1 km north of the Waitahanui mouth. Can be worth exploring during the smelting season and at night. You are unlikely to be disturbed by other anglers.

■ *Waitahanui River mouth:* The most famous river mouth on Lake Taupo, not because of the number of fish caught but because of the 'picket fence' or line of anglers easily viewed from the main highway. This is not the place for a beginner as a long cast with a weight forward medium sinking line is essential if one is to compete with other anglers. After a westerly storm the current will be forced along the beach and 200 m or so can be fished without wading.

The mouth is well known as a place to catch large brown trout, usually during the nights of February and March. Smelt flies are effective during the day and after dark the usual night patterns.

■ *Otupata Creek:* Drains the Rotongaio Lagoon. Good smelt fishing along the beach south of the outlet at the foot of the white cliffs. Worth trying at night.

■ *Hatepe River mouth:* When other rivers are dirty, have a look at the Hatepe. As it drains hydro dams the water remains clear in a fresh. You can drive to the river mouth. Some excellent bags are taken from this mouth.

■ *Waipehi Stream mouth*: There is a delightful rest area beneath kowhai trees at this stream mouth. It is very shallow and rocky. A floating line is essential and there is better fishing after dark. Start well back on the beach as fish move in close to the shore. Fishes well most of the year, even in winter.

■ *Waitetoko Stream mouth*: Comments as for Waipehi Stream (above). Very small stream entering the lake at Manowharangi Bay.

■ *Tauranga-Taupo River mouth*: Before wading and fishing this mouth, it is recommended anglers inspect the area during daylight. This mouth is very deep and dangerous for wading and is generally fished from an anchored boat. The boat is positioned in such a way so as to enable the angler to cast a fly on a heavy sinking line over the very deep lip, pause for a moment and then begin a slow retrieve. Fishing can be excellent at times, generally at night.

SOUTHERN LAKE SHORE
All these streams have easy access. However, as with any new spot, it pays to view the area during daylight before fishing after dark.

■ *Waimarino River mouth*: Can only be fished when the lake is low as a long wade is needed in order to fish over the lip or 'blue line'. At this point the current is barely perceptible and change of position may be necessary before the right spot is found. Use a medium sinking line, cast into deep water and slowly retrieve. A landing net is essential otherwise fish will need to be beached some 100 m behind you.

Fishes well all year but beware of a strong nor'easter. Be confident and carry a length of cord to string fish together on your belt; it may save a long walk when the action is all on.

■ *Waiotaka mouth*: Walk south along the beach from the yacht club and car park. Shallow mouth best fished after dark with a floating line. Has a reputation for brown trout especially after heavy rain when frogs and tadpoles are washed out of the surrounding swamp.

■ *Tongariro mouth or the Delta:* The Delta is a prime fishing spot but can only be reached by boat. Wading along the soft pumice lip is hazardous as the water is 20 m deep. Selecting one of the mouths to fish is governed by the wind direction. The boat should be anchored with the transom barely hanging over the lip. Use a high-density line and a similar technique to that used at the Tauranga-Taupo mouth. Because the water here is deeper a longer interval is advised before beginning the retrieve. The line can be pointing directly beneath the boat. During the day, use a smelt fly, Red Setter or Rabbit pattern, and after dark the usual black night lure. In the winter when trout are entering the river to spawn, fish can even be taken on a Glow Bug or Muppet by the 'heave and leave' method. However, this seems little short of snapper fishing. In favourable conditions, the fishing at the Delta can be quite superb.

■ *Tokaanu tailrace:* Note: fishing is prohibited for 110 m below the powerhouse. From November to February when smelt are running, the screens at the Tokaanu Powerhouse impede their upstream progress. Schools of these tiny fish gather in confusion and are easy prey to marauding trout. Good fly fishing can be obtained from the banks of the tailrace, especially upstream from the main road bridge, although the quality of the surroundings may not equal the quality of the fishing. Weed can cause difficulties at times. However, the tailrace has a reputation for large fish. Fish can also be taken from the Tokaanu wharf and from the mouth of the tailrace close by.

■ *Tokaanu Stream, Slip (Omoho) Creek, Omori and Pukawa streams:* All can be reached from SH 41 between Tokaanu and Kuratau. They should be fished at night with a floating line and smallish night flies. False air casting is strongly recommended and there is room for only two or three rods at each mouth. Little wading is required. Can be fished year round with success. It is illegal to fish these streams except at their mouth.

■ *Kuratau River mouth:* This is a very shallow delta and is safe to wade. Excellent fishing can be had when fish are smelting during the summer. Use a floating line during the day and after dark.

The Kuratau Spit a few hundred metres south of the mouth is well worth fishing as the lip or 'blue line' runs close inshore.

■ *Whareroa River mouth:* Can be reached by car from the Kuratau Hydro road. Use a similar technique as for all shallow river mouths. When the current runs parallel to the shore browns can be caught at night 50 m south of the actual mouth. In the smelting season there is good river mouth and beach fishing.

WESTERN LAKE SHORE
Access is generally by boat.

■ *Whanganui Stream mouth:* This is the most inaccessible of the western bays and generally access is by boat. It is almost 20 km from either Kuratau or Kinloch. Road access through Wharerawa Block is unreliable and at times hazardous because of washouts in the pumice road. A four-wheel-drive vehicle is very useful. Over the past few years the river mouth has become too shallow for sheltering a boat. There is very good stream mouth and beach fishing during the smelting season. A medium sinking or floating line is recommended. If the action is slow at the rip, try at the southern end of the beach close to the bush. Trout follow smelt along the rocky shore.

■ *Waikino Stream mouth:* Gushes out of a rocky cleft between Whanganui and Waihaha bays. There is a peg to tie a boat to on the north side. A heavy sinking line is needed to reach fish clearly visible deep beneath the current.

Occasionally, night fishing can be excellent at this spot, even off the rocky shelf on the southern side.

■ *Waihaha River mouth:* Access is by boat; the nearest boat ramp is Kinloch. The bay can also be reached by walking down a steep track through bush from the end of Waihaha Road off SH 32. Although the mouth changes during storms, it usually remains sufficiently deep to shelter a boat. Fishing is best when the current flows in the direction of Whakatonga (Richwhite) Point. When fish are smelting, exciting fishing can be had from the point itself, especially if a mate sits high on the hill and spots. Beach fishing for smelting fish is good in November and December.

Two or three kilometres upstream are the Tieke Falls. They can be reached by a small boat and the falls pool offers good fishing.

■ *Otupoto Falls:* Enter the lake at the southern end of Waihora Bay. Fly casting from a boat can be done although the usual method of fishing is trolling.

■ *Waihora River mouth:* Access is by boat from Kinloch. There is a good, sheltered anchorage close by in Boat Harbour at Kawakawa Point. Excellent night fishing can be had at this mouth and fish smelt along the beach in November and December.

Large brown trout often lie deep in the lower reaches of this river but are very wary and difficult to catch.

■ *Chinaman's Creek (Tutaeuaua Creek):* Enters the southern end of Kawakawa Bay. A private four-wheel-drive track leads off Whangamata Road to the clifftop, and there is a walking track down through the bush to the stream mouth, ten minutes' to the north. Usual methods apply to this shallow mouth. Holds two rods comfortably.

Northern lake shore

- *Otakitaki Stream mouth:* Can only be reached when the lake is low by wading round a rocky point at the western end of Whangamata Bay.

- *Whangamata Stream mouth:* Reached by walking west along the beach from Kinloch.

- *Mapara Stream mouth:* Enters the eastern end of Whakaipo Bay. This mouth is very popular and heavily fished. A strong southerly or westerly wind will make it unfishable. Floating or sink tip line, false air casting and the usual night flies should bring reward providing there are not too many rods present. Then the angler with the longest cast has the best chance of success. The eastern shoreline of Whakaipo Bay south of the Mapara mouth also fishes well.

Rivers flowing into Lake Taupo

Waitahanui River

■ *Access*

From SH 1 and side roads Mill Road and Blake Road.

Because it is spring fed, this medium-sized river has a consistent flow and seldom discolours. The river bed is fine pumice and the banks are stable. As the water is deep and quite swift, nymphing can be difficult in some stretches and the deeply sunk lure accounts for the majority of fish taken. Successful anglers use a high-density line and a slow retrieve. Many bury their rod tip in the river to ensure the fly swims through the lies.

The best fishing can be had in March through to September and after a good southerly storm, scores of fish enter the river. These can easily be seen from the main road bridge. This river is not for the faint-hearted and often, because of the intense angling pressure, fishing ethics have largely disappeared. Above the bridge there are 7 km of good water with well-formed pools, and anglers find less pressure in these upper reaches.

A wide variety of flies is used including Parson's Glory, Red Setter, Rabbit variations and smelt patterns. We have found a size 4–6 Orange Rabbit with a long tail to be a good teaser but a friend swears by a Green Smelt. The crucial factors for success are probably not the fly but the depth and the way it swims through the lie and whether the river is holding fresh-run trout.

Hatepe or Hinemaiaia River

NOTE: The river is closed above the main road bridge from 31 May to 1 December. Fishing is not permitted within 300 m of the lower dam. There is a sign at this point.

■ *Above the bridge*

There is superb nymph water in this small stream although overhanging vegetation can make casting tricky in places.

Hooked fish also have a chance to escape by tangling round snags. Fluctuations in water flow resulting from hydro-electric operations have caused some bank erosion and deterioration in recent years. Use a trace measuring roughly 4 m and false cast. In shallow lies, endeavour to land the nymph well above sighted fish, with the line behind. In the deeper pools, fish are not so easily frightened and lining the fish may not be detrimental. Many nymph patterns will take fish but the smaller sizes are more effective. Try Pheasant Tail, Hare and Copper, White Caddis, and Half Back patterns all weighted and in sizes 12–14.

■ *Below the bridge*
The water is more suited to sunk downstream lure methods. Lures can also be very effective above the bridge especially after a fresh run. Try Rabbit flies, Smelt patterns, Red Setter and Parson's Glory in sizes 6–8 on a medium sinking line.

TAURANGA-TAUPO RIVER
NOTE: Above the Rangers' Pool where the Mangakowhitiwhiti Stream enters, the river is closed from 31 May to 1 December.

■ *Access*
Quarry Road from SH 1 crosses private land on the true right bank. This road beyond the crescent is now unserviceable, even for four-wheel-drive vehicles. There are good tracks on both sides of the river. Care is required at the Cliff Pool ford when the river is high.

This delightful medium-sized river is recommended for novices as wading is safe on a shingle bed and casting is generally unimpeded by vegetation.

Fish run from April to September, as is the case with all Taupo rivers, and the most productive time to fish is after a storm and heavy rain. During fine weather and low-water conditions, the fishing can be hard. There are well-defined pools and runs.

We remember a day in August when heavy rain began at midday breaking a long dry spell. By evening, the river had risen to cover the car park at the end of the quarry road. The river was unfishable but trout were running up the edge of the muddy torrent in great numbers, even in the grass. Next morning the river level had dropped and the fishing was superb.

The river can be fished after dark but few anglers take advantage of this. Weighted nymphs and Glow Bugs take their share of fish. In the deeper pools such as the Rangers', Windmill and Cliff, lies tend to be towards the tail of the pool. When lure fishing, cast well across the pool with a sinking line and wait twenty seconds before commencing the retrieve. The lure should then swim deeply through the lie. Pools can also be fished with one or two well-weighted nymphs on a 4.5–5 m trace and a floating line. Darker fish spawning should be returned and only fresh-run fish kept.

Use the same flies and nymphs as for the Hatepe with the addition of Bug Eye, Muppet, Glow Bug, Dappled Dog, Jock Miller, Mrs Simpson and the usual night flies.

After 1 December, good dry fly and nymph fishing can be obtained on mending fish especially in runs above the Rangers' Pool. The upper gorge provides a challenge for the adventurous angler in summer although access off Kiko Road can be a problem unless a motorbike is used.

WAIMARINO RIVER

NOTE: Closed season above Korohe Crossing from 31 May to 1 December.

■ *Access*
Lower reaches from SH 1 just south of Motuoapa. There is a vehicle access track up the true left bank.
Middle and upper reaches from Korohe Road.

A small river which fishes much better after a fresh and when there is a good volume of water in the river. Below SH 1 the

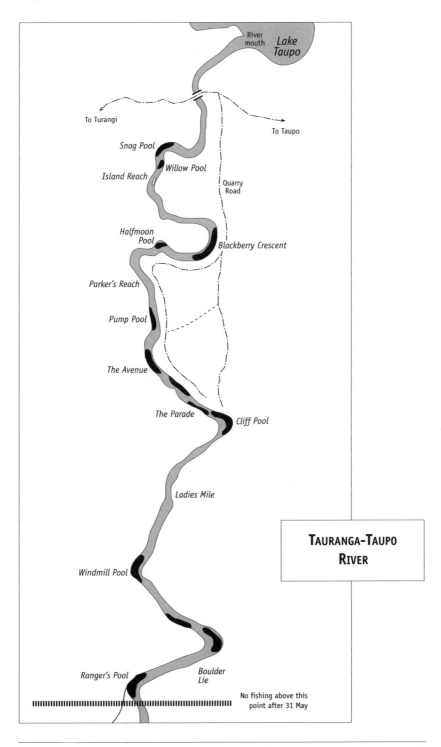

River mouth

Lake Taupo

To Turangi

To Taupo

Snag Pool

Willow Pool

Island Reach

Quarry Road

Halfmoon Pool

Blackberry Crescent

Parker's Reach

Pump Pool

The Avenue

The Parade

Cliff Pool

Ladies Mile

TAURANGA-TAUPO RIVER

Windmill Pool

Ranger's Pool

Boulder Lie

No fishing above this point after 31 May

river is overgrown with willows. Up to the Korohe Crossing there are a few holding pools which are well worth fishing. Fish can easily be spotted and just as easily disturbed. Above Korohe Pa there is excellent water but fish are wary and need to be approached cautiously.

The upper reaches hold a few resident fish for the energetic angler prepared to walk long distances. The usual lures and nymphs are effective but as the river is small and clear, use the smaller sizes.

Waiotaka Stream

NOTE: Above the Hautu Ford, fishing is permitted from 1 December to 31 May.

■ *Access*
The lower reaches can be reached from the Hautu Pa road. The middle and upper reaches can be fished by courtesy of the Department of Justice. Arrangements can be made through the Superintendent of Hautu Prison as the stream flows through the prison grounds.

A smaller but similar stream to the upper Waimarino, and fishing methods are the same. The lower reaches hold fish after a fresh. The pools are small, but fish lie deep and under overhanging banks. The stretch running through the prison is ideal nymphing water.

Tongariro River

■ *Access*
Generally good as the river is well tracked by the Department of Conservation. Above the main road bridge, SH 1 follows the true left bank from Turangi to the Poutu River. At the Poutu bridge there is a shingle road giving access to the upper pools — Breakaway, Fan, Boulder, Blue, Sand, Whitikau and Fence. There is vehicle access off SH 1 to the Red Hut Pool, the Birch Pools (through the hatchery), Kamahi and the old Admiral's Pools and off Taupehi Road to

the Hydro, Breakfast, Major Jones, Island and Judges Pool. The Lonely and Bridge pools lie either side of the main road bridge. Below the Bridge, Grace Road follows the true right bank downstream from SH 1 giving access to the Stones (off Herekiekie Street), Bain, Log, Reed, Jones, the Parade, Smallman's Reach, DeLatours and Graces. Access to the true left bank below the main road bridge can be obtained from Turangi township.

Begg's Pool below the hydro dam can be approached from the Desert Road on the Kaimanawa Forest Park Road. This is a launching place for rafting, and anglers fishing the Whitikau, Sand and Blue pools are often disturbed by rafts.

■ *Season*
Above the Fence Pool 1 December–31 May.
Elsewhere, open all year.

Many excellent books have been written about this world-famous river describing the pools in considerable detail. Despite reduced water flows taken for power generation, the river still deserves its reputation.

Below the main road bridge, the river is shingly and willowed. Above the bridge, the scenery improves with clumps of manuka and native bush softening the river. Nymph fishing predominates in the upper river while lure fishing is more popular in the Major Jones Pool and below the bridge. Both methods can be equally effective in all parts of the river, but lure fishing tends to be hard during fine weather and reduced water flows.

The river can be crossed at certain spots but great care should be taken as the rocks can be slippery with algae and the current is swift. Pools can change significantly during floods and lies that were productive prior to the flood may become barren and silt laden. This has occurred to some extent recently in the Whitikau and Island pools. The Lonely Pool has almost disappeared. Try the Hydro Pool on the true right bank near the mouth of the Mangamawhitiwhiti

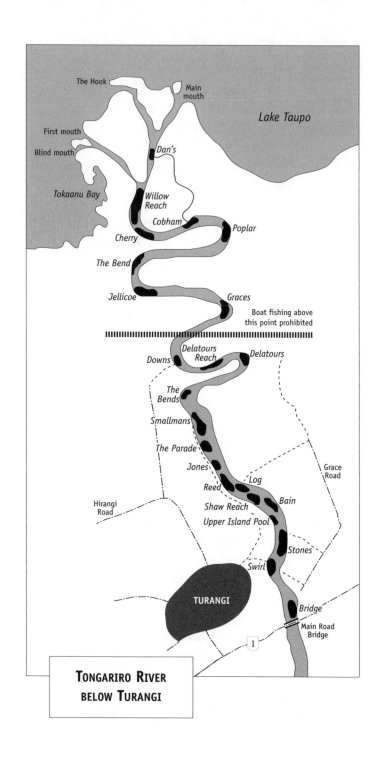

The Hook

Main mouth

Lake Taupo

First mouth

Blind mouth

Dan's

Tokaanu Bay

Willow Reach

Cobham

Cherry

Poplar

The Bend

Jellicoe

Graces

Boat fishing above
this point prohibited

Delatours Reach

Downs

Delatours

The Bends

Smallmans

The Parade

Jones

Log

Grace Road

Reed

Hirangi Road

Shaw Reach

Bain

Upper Island Pool

Stones

Swirl

TURANGI

Bridge

Main Road Bridge

1

**TONGARIRO RIVER
BELOW TURANGI**

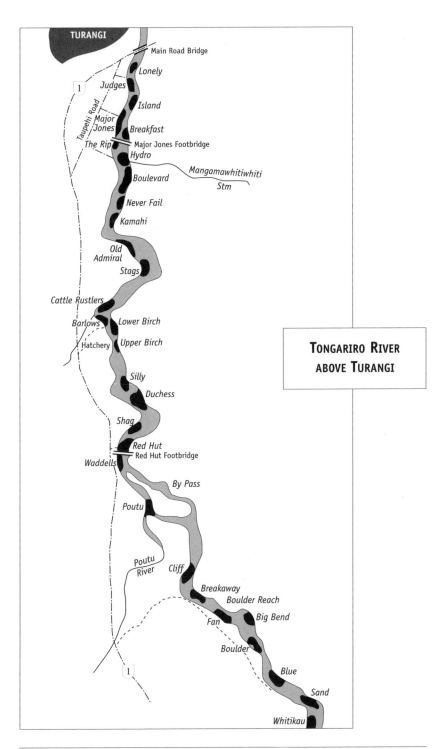

TURANGI

Main Road Bridge

Lonely

Judges

1

Island

Major
Jones

Breakfast

The Rip

Major Jones Footbridge

Hydro

Boulevard

Mangamawhitiwhiti
Stm

Never Fail

Kamahi

Old
Admiral

Stags

Cattle Rustlers

Barlows

Lower Birch

Hatchery

Upper Birch

Silly

Duchess

Shag

Red Hut

Red Hut Footbridge

Waddells

By Pass

Poutu

Poutu
River

Cliff

Breakaway

Boulder Reach

Fan

Big Bend

Boulder

Blue

Sand

Whitikau

**TONGARIRO RIVER
ABOVE TURANGI**

Stream for large brownies. You will need to be on the river early to obtain this favourite spot. The angling pressure on some of these pools is intense but do not be discouraged when your favourite stretch of river is fully occupied as most pools and runs hold fish, especially after a fresh. Seek out some of the unlikely spots and you could be pleasantly surprised.

In the warm summer months, good dry fly fishing can be enjoyed on mending fish and there is little angling pressure at this time of the year. Try an imitation sedge and skim it across the surface of a pool. Large brown trout can be stalked in the slow-flowing lower reaches below Delatours Pool.

■ *Etiquette*
To avoid unpleasant confrontations which can ruin a day's fishing, always ask another angler fishing the pool where you can start fishing. It may be obvious if others are all nymphing; you can join the queue downstream. Similarly, if others are all downstream lure fishing, start at the top of the pool. However, problems arise when an angler is fishing a Glow Bug downstream on a sinking line.

Trolling and harling
More fish are taken in Taupo from a boat than by any other method. Remember, it is illegal to troll or harl within 300 m of any stream or river mouth. The only exceptions are the Waikino and Otupoto Falls.

■ *Launching facilities*
Small boats can be launched from most beaches. There are boat ramps for larger boats at Taupo on the Waikato River outlet, at Acacia Bay, Kinloch, Kuratau Spit, Waihi, Tokaanu Wharf, Motuoapa and at Four Mile Bay or Wharewaka.

■ *Safety advice*
Maori sometimes called the lake Taupo-hau-rau — 'Lake of a hundred winds' — because of the strong southerly winds that can spring up unexpectedly. A short, steep 1.5 m chop

Tongariro River

can prove troublesome even for a 5 m boat and a 60 hp outboard. Anglers are advised to carry the same safety equipment as if fishing offshore at sea.

■ *Harling a fly*
When fish are smelting from September to February, harling a smelt fly on a fly rod and a high-density line can be most effective. Boat speed must be kept to a minimum either by using a small auxiliary outboard motor or slowing down the boat by towing a 'sea anchor'. Let out the whole length of fly line and 20 m of backing to ensure the fly sinks sufficiently. The trace should be 5–6 m long.

Favoured flies include Parson's Glory, Ginger Mick, Orange, Yellow and Green Rabbit, Taupo Tiger, Grey Ghost and other smelt varieties, Hamill's Killer, Green and Yellow Orbit in sizes 4–6.

Trolling a spinner

In the autumn (fall) and winter trout become bottom feeders and trolling a spinner on a wire or lead line along the drop-off or 'blue line' brings results. The wire line will sink deeper than the lead line but is more difficult to handle and tangles readily. Do not turn the boat too sharply when using either of these lines. Downriggers became legal in the 1994–95 season. The maximum line length permitted on the reel drum is 40m. These enable anglers to use a monofilament line at the required depth. Fish fight more enthusiastically on light gear, especially when not towing a length of heavy lead or wire line.

When a fish is caught, turn the boat and troll over the same area. If using a monofilament line, it pays to let out 80–100 m. The breaking strain should be 8–9 kg. Some anglers attach a length of lead line to the monofilament. With a lead line, experiment using different lengths in order to find the optimum depth. A number of colours can be used as a measurement and guide once this has been found. Trout can also be taken by jigging.

ABOVE: A 4WD with a camper is a great way to get around

LEFT: Which fly?

Whanganui Bay, Lake Taupo

Careful spotting is easier from a height

Hot spot — where snow melt meets clear water

Difficult lumpy tussock banks make spotting difficult

Careful stalking on the Mary Burn

Trophy brown trout from a West Coast river

Accurate presentation required

ABOVE: Fast to a good fish

LEFT: Success on a high country lake

Catch and release

Clear water is deceptive when crossing

Managing a lively fish in pocket water, Ruakituri River

Favoured spinners include Toby, Cobra, Flatfish and Zed Spinners of varying colours and sizes.

■ *Favoured trolling locations*
Trout can be caught anywhere in the lake, even in the middle, but good areas include Whanganui Bay, Kawakawa Bay, Whangamata Bay, the Whakaipo Reef, Mine Bay, Rangatira Point, off the Waitahanui mouth and the Horomatangi Reef located off Rotongaio.

Spinning in Lake Taupo
Spinning is only permitted in the lake. There is no spinning permitted in any of the streams flowing into Lake Taupo nor within 300 m of any stream mouth.

Few anglers use this method in Taupo but for a young angler learning to fish, spinning is easier to start with than a fly. All three varieties of reel (closed and open-faced spinning reel and baitcasting reel) can be used. Apart from the spinner, no added weights may be employed. During the smelting season, a small bright silvery spinner can be most effective.

LAKE ROTOAIRA
■ *Licence*
Taupo plus a special licence from the Maori owners of the lake. The lake is privately owned. The season opens on 1 September and closes on 30 June.

■ *Location*
SH 47 circles the southern shores while Te Ponanga Saddle Road from Turangi and SH 41 skirts the northern shore.

■ *Access*
Boat launching facilities at the Rotoaira Fishing Camp and for small boats at the foot of Te Ponanga Saddle near the tailrace and at the Wairehu Canal.

Bag limit is eight fish.

Boat fishing, either harling a fly, trolling a spinner or fly casting from a drifting boat is necessary as the shoreline is swampy and difficult. Only rainbow are present and stocks are high with fish averaging 1–2 kg.

Fly casting is probably the most productive method and flies used include Hamill's Killer, Kilwell varieties, Rabbit flies and Red Setter. Use a medium sinking line. Best fished from February to May. The size and abundance of fish has been reduced by the alteration in lake water flow as a result of hydro development.

There is good fly fishing at the mouth of the Wairehu Canal off the rocky groynes. The groynes at the Poutu end of the lake are also worth a try.

LAKE OTAMANGAKAU

■ *Location and access*
On the opposite side of Te Ponanga Saddle Road to Lake Rotoaira (SH 47). Two access roads are signposted to Wanganui intake, Te Whaiau Dam, Otamangakau Dam, boat ramp, and Wairehu Control Gate.

■ *Season*
1 October–30 June.

The headwaters of the Whanganui River were diverted to form this lake in 1971 as part of the Tongariro power scheme. The lake is surrounded by flat tussock country and scrub but the view of the mountains in the Tongariro National Park certainly adds to its scenic qualities.

The 'Big O' covers an area of 150 ha and holds some magnificent trout. Rainbows predominate and fish over 6 kg have been taken. Trout food in the lake is plentiful and consists of dragonfly and damsel larvae, mayflies, caddis, snails and midge larvae. There are no smelt or bullies in this lake. All legal methods can be used but the majority of fish are caught from boats or float tubes either harling a lure or fly casting a lure, nymph or dry fly.

Traditional lure fishing from the shore with either a slow or fast sinking line is effective as is nymph fishing with a floater. Trolling a spinner or spin fishing from the shore is difficult because of the weed banks. The lake is subject to wide fluctuations in water level and for this reason conditions can change rapidly. It can also discolour after heavy rain.

Try a Hamill's Killer, an Orange Rabbit or a large black fly at night, especially near the Wairehu Canal outlet. With the floater, use a very slow retrieve and a Dragon Fly or Half Back nymph or a Woolly Bugger. Even an imitation cicada can be deadly in windy summer conditions. Trout will often smash

Lake Otamangakau

the cicada without initially taking it. Leave it on the water until the trace begins to move away as the fish may well return and take it on the second attempt. In the evening, fish will rise to a Twilight Beauty or Royal Wulff. Be prepared for large, superb-conditioned fish that strip 50–70 m of line off your reel and then bury themselves deep in a weed bed. You are doing well if you hook three to four fish in a day and land only one of them. Trout taste like the snails they feed on so catch and release is recommended.

Ngaruroro River

Isolated rivers east of Taupo

Three inaccessible rivers, the Rangitikei, Ngaruroro and Mohaka, drain the Kaimanawa and Kaweka Forest Parks east of Taupo and Turangi. A New Zealand licence is required for these rivers.

Rangitikei River (upper reaches)

■ *Location and access*

There is vehicle access to limited water from the Taihape-Napier Road provided one is prepared to walk, ford a medium-sized river and tramp. There is a basic campsite where the Taihape-Napier Road crosses the Rangitikei, a 45-minute drive from Taihape. Otherwise, aside from difficult back country tramping, access to the favoured upper reaches is by helicopter from Taupo, Turangi or Taihape.

■ *Season*

1 October to 30 April.

Bag limit upstream of Springvale Bridge on the Taihape-Napier Road to the Oturua Stream confluence is two trout. Above Oturua Stream the bag limit is one fish. Catch and release is strongly advised for this section of river.

This magnificent, large, wild and scenic river with a reputation for trophy fish offers 30 km of excellent water above Springvale Bridge. There is plenty of fly fishing below this bridge but the upper reaches offer the best sight fishing. Overseas anglers and their guides frequently visit this river but fishing is not easy. Although the water clarity is excellent and fish can be spotted, they are wary and often lie at the tail of very deep pools. Rainbow up to 7 kg predominate but there are also some very large browns. Native bush lines the banks˙above the Mangamaire tributary whereas 3 km below this confluence the river enters barren tussock country. In warm summer conditions trout can be stalked on the edges of runs and pools with a dry fly or nymph. However, many fish lying in deep water can only be caught by floating heavily weighted nymphs down to them on a sinking line. Occasionally these fish will also accept a well-sunk Woolly Bugger, Yellow Rabbit or Red Setter.

Provided the river has been assessed during the day, night fishing in deep pools with a well-sunk black lure can be very exciting. This is a wonderful river to fish on a warm sunny day but anglers should be aware that this is a very cold valley and snow can fall on the tops at any time of the year.

The Mangamaire tributary offers another 15 km of high quality back country fishing for sighted fish but a lot of hard walking and river crossings are required.

NGARURORO RIVER (UPPER REACHES)

■ *Location and access*
There is another campsite at Kuripapango on the Ngaruroro River one-and-a-half-hour's drive from Taihape on the Taihape-Napier Road. There is a fixed wing airstrip to the upper Ngaruroro at Boyd Hut. Large stretches of this river can be reached only by experienced trampers or by helicopter.

■ *Season*
1 October to 31 May.

Only the river upstream from Kuripapango on the Taihape-Napier Road can be highly recommended for fly fishing.

There is reasonable fishing in the lower reaches but the middle reaches below Kuripapango are very gorgy and inaccessible.

At the Boyd Hut and airstrip, the river flows through tussock and scrub. Fourteen kilometres below the Boyd, this clear, medium-sized mountain river enters native bush. The best stretch of water naturally lies in the most inaccessible country between Cameron Hut and Gold (Panoko) Creek. There is a rough trampers' track upstream from Kuripapango which can be followed to Cameron Hut (three and a half hours). The river can only be fished upstream from Kuri-papango in low-water conditions as there are some waist-high crossings. Holds both rainbow and brown trout up to 4 kg which can be spotted in bright conditions. This river is similar to the Rangitikei as both are very clear with deep pools. If fish are feeding they can be spotted on the edges and will respond to carefully presented dry flies or nymphs.

MOHAKA RIVER

■ *Location*
The Oamaru, Kaipo and Taharua rivers join in the Kai-manawa Forest Park to form the upper Mohaka River. The main river then flows southeast for over 20 km through the Kaweka Forest Park before meeting the Ripia River near Pakaututu. From Pakaututu the river turns northeast and eventually reaches the Pacific Ocean south of Wairoa at Mohaka.

■ *Access to upper reaches*
• By fixed wing plane from Taupo to private airstrips, that is Oamaru, 'Footy Field' and Otupua.
• By tramping for six hours over Te Iringa Saddle from SH 5 and Clements access road.
• By helicopter.
• Private access through Poronui but only for anglers staying at the lodge.

■ *Access to middle reaches*
• At Pakaututu north of Puketitiri.
• From SH 5 which crosses the river 45 km north of Napier and then from McVicars Road or Waitara Road.
• Willow Flat Road leaves SH 2 near Kotemaori.

This large, wild and scenic river is difficult to access but well worth fishing. The upper reaches flow through tussock, scrub and bush but the river can be crossed and waded. Below Otupua, the river banks become overgrown with scrub and bush lawyer making progress difficult. Some angler-hunters raft this section but it takes three days to reach SH 5 bridge. Good stocks of rainbow and brown trout averaging 1.5 kg provide excellent sport. Fish can be spotted and stalked with nymphs or dry flies.

Below Pakaututu the river becomes large although it can still be crossed at selected fords in low-water conditions. Trout can be spotted when feeding along the edges but many anglers fish to rising fish or fish blind. Below Willow Flat the river is best suited to spinning.

Most well-weighted nymphs will take fish as will sedge, mayfly and attractor pattern dry flies. Accurate presentation is more important than fly pattern, especially in the upper reaches.

WAIRARAPA DISTRICT

Wairarapa lies in the southeast of the North Island, a one-and-a-half-hour drive from the capital city Wellington. It is bordered by the rugged Tararua Mountains to the west and the Pacific Ocean to the east. Summers are warm and dry.

There is a wide variety of exciting outdoor activities, interesting shops and museums in the small country towns and excellent wineries in the Martinborough area. Golfers are well catered for with good courses in Masterton, Carterton and Martinborough. As the Wairarapa is also renowned for its gardens and nurseries, they are well worth a visit.

Accommodation includes budget backpackers, camping grounds and cabins, homestays and farmstays, bed and breakfasts, motels with facilities and hotels. Additionally, there are luxury lodges, country houses and rural retreats.

The Mount Bruce National Wildlife Centre, 25 minutes north of Masterton, displays live takahe, kiwi, kokako and tuatara. The Wairarapa coast is wild and rugged but there are great walks and the Tararua Forest Park also offers scenic tramps and bush walks.

There are sports stores in most small country towns where local angling information can be obtained. However, fly selection may be limited.

More information can be obtained from:

Tourism Wairarapa
PO Box 814, Masterton
Ph 06 378 7373
Fax 06 378 7042

WAIRARAPA RIVERS

MANAWATU RIVER

■ *Location*

This popular large river drains southern Hawke's Bay, the southern Ruahine Range and the northern Tararua Range. The main river follows a southerly course to Dannevirke, where it turns east and enters the Manawatu Gorge 8 km east of Woodville. It emerges near Ashhurst, meanders across farmland to Palmerston North and reaches the sea at Foxton Beach. Only the middle and upper reaches above the Manawatu Gorge are recommended.

■ *Access*

Roads follow the river quite closely throughout most of its course. Permission is required to cross private farmland. Some of the suggested roads to take include: Kopua Road, which leaves SH 2 just south of the Manawatu Bridge between Takapau and Norsewood; Garfield Road 19 km north of Dannevirke, to Makotuku, then on Donghi or Rakaitai roads; Oringi Road 10 km south of Dannevirke.

■ *Season*

Upstream of its confluence with the Mangatewainui Stream near Ormondville, 1 October to 30 April. Elsewhere 1 October to 30 September.

Above Dannevirke there is excellent fly water. The river lies east of SH 2 and the upper reaches cross the highway just north of Norsewood. Fish can be spotted and stalked with dry fly and nymph, and brown trout up to 2 kg are not uncommon. There are good pools and runs through willows and farmland. The river is not too large and can be waded and crossed. Eutrophication can cause problems in hot summer conditions. The banks are generally clear for casting.

The stretch of water between Oringi and Dannevirke contains a very high fish population. The river here has a

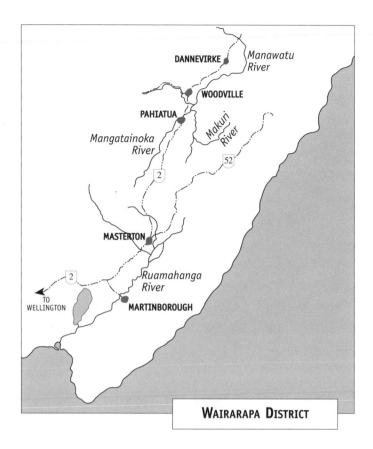

WAIRARAPA DISTRICT

shingle and mud bed with large, deep pools, long glides and wide shingly riffles. Trout are difficult to spot but wading is safe. Crossings are possible at the tail of pools providing care is taken. There is good sedge fishing on warm summer evenings using a soft-hackle wet fly or a deer-hair sedge. Emerger patterns can prove deadly.

Downstream of Woodville the water is heavy and better suited to wet-fly fishing and spinning.

MANGATAINOKA RIVER

■ *Location*
Flows parallel to and between SH 2 in the east and the Mangahao River in the west. Enters the Manawatu south of Woodville near Ngawapurua.

Upper Manawatu River

■ *Access*

Road access west of SH 2 at successive turn-offs to Mangamutu, at Konini, to Mangamaire and to Hukanui from Hamua. The Mangatainoka Valley Road can be reached west of Eketahuna. SH 2 crosses the river at Mangatainoka close by the DB brewery.

■ *Season*

Above the Makakahi confluence, 1 October to 30 April. Elsewhere 1 October to 30 September. Above the road bridge on the Hamua-Hukanui Road, fly fishing only.

This large river is highly rated by anglers and heavily fished. The river has been protected by a conservation order and fish stocks are good. The river bed is shingle and the low, willow-lined banks generally permit unobstructed fly casting on one side of the river. There are well-defined pools and long glides. Crossings are generally not difficult although the stony bed can be slippery. There is approximately 45 km of fishable water. The middle and lower reaches are the most productive and hold slightly larger fish than the upper reaches. Above Hukanui, the river is unstable and prone to changing course in floods. Following the onset of warm temperatures most of the trout drop back downstream.

There is often a good evening rise and fish can be spotted and stalked in the middle to upper reaches. There is excellent water adjacent to the DB brewery. Try size 12 to 14 Pheasant Tail, Half Back, Hare's Ear or Midge Pupa nymphs during the day, along with Coch-y-bondhu, Adams and Dad's Favourite dry flies. In the evening it is hard to go past Twilight Beauty in sizes 12 to 14 or a deer-hair sedge. Softhackle wet flies are very effective. Browns in the 0.75–2 kg range can be expected.

MAKURI RIVER

■ *Location*
Drains the Waewaepa and Puketoi ranges east of Pahiatua. The river flows in a southwesterly direction but just south of Makuri turns north to enter the Tiraumea River at Ngaturi.

■ *Access*
East of Pahiatua on the Ngaturi-Makuri Road.

■ *Season*
1 October to 30 April. Above the Makuri township bridge, fly fishing only.

This is a small tributary of the Tiraumea River highly rated by fly anglers. Some years ago, Hardy's of London named one of their fly rods after this river, such was its reputation. The most popular stretch lies in the region of Makuri village, where the willow-lined stream wanders across farmland. Trout are easily spotted and just as easily frightened, so a careful approach and fine tippets are essential for success. This is especially true after Christmas due to the high

Makuri River

concentration of anglers over the holiday season. Early morning is often the best time to fish. Fish fight well and have a tendency to tangle in the willow roots. One kilometre upstream from the domain the river is more difficult to fish because of overhanging scrub. Downstream, in the region of the gorge, limestone sink holes, large boulders and native bush provide considerable interest for the fit angler. Boots and shorts are recommended for this rough piece of water, but there are some large browns. Try a well-weighted stonefly nymph. Good fishing continues for 1 km below the gorge, then the river becomes sluggish and uninteresting. Although some anglers believe this river has deteriorated over the past twenty years, drift dives by Fish and Game Council officers have been reassuring and some excellent fish up to 3 kg have been seen. As a result of clear-felling in the headwaters, this river easily becomes silt laden in a fresh. There is basic camping in the Makuri Domain with an even more basic golf course.

RUAMAHANGA RIVER

■ *Location*
Rises in the Tararua Range northwest of Masterton, flows in a southerly direction just east of Masterton and empties into Lake Onoke at Palliser Bay.

■ *Access to upper reaches*
Flows parallel to but east of SH 2 from Mount Bruce to Masterton. The stretch in the bush-covered Tararua Range can only be reached by tramping across private farmland (permission required).

■ *Access to middle reaches*
From the Masterton-Gladstone Road. From Papawai and Morrisons Bush southeast of Greytown. From Martinborough.

■ *Access to lower reaches*
From the Martinborough-Lake Ferry Road.

■ *Season*
Open season from 1 October to 30 September.

A river popular with anglers because of the good catch rate, large area of fishable water and easy access. This large river has a wide shingle bed with long glides and riffles. Willows line the banks in some stretches but wading is safe. Near Masterton there are cliffs.

The middle reaches are the most heavily fished and brown trout weighing 0.5–3 kg can be taken equally on fly, spinner and live bait. This river is well stocked and in favourable conditions an excellent evening rise occurs. Recently rainbow trout up to 1.5 kg have been caught around Masterton and downstream to Gladstone. It is thought these may have escaped from Henley Lake in Masterton which has been stocked for junior anglers.

Favoured locations include Wardells Bridge east of Masterton, the cliffs area just south of Masterton, Te Whiti Bridge and Ponatahi Bridge. In the headwaters above Mount Bruce there is always the chance of a trophy fish. From Mount Bruce downstream to Masterton the river is very unstable and subject to shingle extraction. Below Tuhitarata the river is deep, slow flowing and sluggish, but local anglers are achieving results by slow trolling the river. A few large sea-run browns up to 6 kg enter the river during February and March but these are hard to catch. Perch up to 1.5 kg are present in the river up as far as Masterton and will take any variety of trout lure.

In a fresh the river rapidly becomes silt laden and takes time to clear. Try Caddis, Red-tipped Governor, Willow Grub and Dark Hare and Copper (Hare's Ear) nymphs, Dad's Favourite, Parachute Adams, Coch-y-bondhu and Twilight Beauty dry flies or Hamill's Killer and small Yellow Rabbit lures. For the spin angler, Veltic, Meps and Cobra take fish. The lower reaches are generally fished with spinning gear, while the upper reaches offer good fishing for the adventurous fly angler prepared to walk.

There are many other smaller streams and tributaries of the rivers described above that are worth exploring also. These include the upper reaches of the Waiohine and Waingawa, the Makakahi and the Kopuaranga rivers; also the Kourarau Dam. For additional information, we suggest checking at the local sports stores or referring to the *North Island Trout Fishing Guide* by John Kent.

NELSON DISTRICT

With high sunshine hours, warm safe beaches and beautiful landscapes, the small city of Nelson (population 35 000) is a favourite destination for both local and overseas holiday-makers. A relaxed lifestyle has attracted potters, artists, woodturners and glassblowers, and their crafts are exhibited in a number of fascinating galleries. There is a wide range of intriguing restaurants and 'cruisy' cafes all waiting to serve visitors and locals alike. Nelson scallops are notable and the seasonal, locally grown berry fruits should not be over-looked.

Major events in the area include the Nelson Jazz Festival (December 27–31), the Gentle Annie Craft Fair (January 1), the Air New Zealand Mardi Gras featuring live music (January 10), and Taste Nelson, the food/wine/beerfest (January 26).

Outdoor activities in this region are extensive and encompass caving, sea kayaking, golfing, hiking, skydiving, horse trekking, sea fishing, diving, yachting, and rock climbing. Tramping the Abel Tasman, Kahurangi and Nelson Lakes National Parks is a favourite venture for the fit and active. Wine tours through noteworthy local vineyards or visiting boutique breweries should be high on the list of priorities when not angling. In addition, some historic homes and gardens are worth consideration.

Accommodation of every description is available but advance booking is advisable during the high holiday season (mid-December to mid-March).

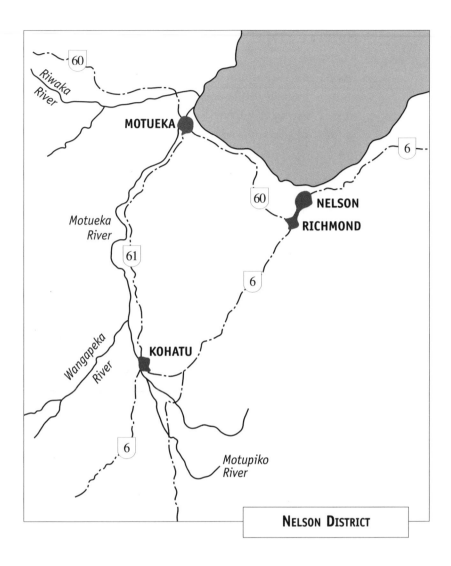

Fly shops with respectable inventory are located in town and professional guides are available for hire. As the demand may be high over the summer months we suggest booking well in advance.

For more information contact:

Tourism Nelson
PO Box 788, Nelson
Ph 03 546 6228
Fax 03 546 9008

MOTUEKA RIVER

■ *Location*

Drains the Richmond Range to the east, the Hope and Lookout Ranges to the south and the Arthur Range to the west. Flows in a northerly direction from the Motupiko-Tadmor districts, through Ngatimoti to enter Tasman Bay just north of Motueka.

■ *Access*

The river is well serviced with roads on both sides of the river from the Golden Downs Forest to its mouth near Motueka some 60 km away. SH 61 follows the river upstream on the east bank from Motueka to SH 6 at Kohatu. There are a number of marked public accesses and the river can also be approached across private farmland, providing prior permission is obtained. A detailed access map can be obtained from the Nelson/Marlborough Fish and Game Council.

■ *Season*

Downstream from the Ngatimoti Bridge, the river is open all year. Elsewhere, 1 October to 30 April.

■ *Restrictions*

Below SH 6 bridge at Kohatu, the bag limit is four trout; above this bridge, two trout, but only one fish exceeding 50 cm.

Despite being very popular and heavily fished, this river holds an abundance of brown trout averaging around 1 kg, although fish up to 2.5 kg are occasionally taken. Fish stocks equal any other river in New Zealand (275 fish/km at Woodstock). The river is wide and offers long glides and ripples flowing over a stable, shingle bed which can be easily waded in most areas. There are also some very deep holding pools. The banks are willow-lined but present no great obstruction to casting. Fish can be spotted in some areas, but the fish population is so high that any pool or run is

Motueka River

likely to hold fish and can therefore be fished blind. During the day try a small (sizes 16–18) Coch-y-bondhu, Adams, Dad's Favourite or Royal Wulff. Any small, lightly weighted nymph is effective in the shallow water, while a heavier nymph should be used for the deeper runs. There is a good evening rise during summer and fish respond to mayfly imitations such as Kakahi Queen and Twilight Beauty in sizes 14–18. At dusk we have had success with a small dark sedge or a small sparsely tied wet fly such as Twilight Beauty, Purple Grouse, Alder or March Brown fished either upstream or across and swung with the current on a floating line. Fish tend to take these flies just when they start to speed up on the swing. Sensitivity is called for with this method. Unless the line is tightened immediately when the fish takes, the deception will be rapidly ejected. This is a great river for the angler learning the art of fly fishing.

The spin angler should use a small Veltic, a gold or silver Toby or a Meps and fish the deeper runs under the willows. As is usually the case, fishing with a spinner is better after a fresh.

There is a good camping ground at Alexander Bluff's

Bridge 10 km south of Motueka. One can spend a very enjoyable holiday on this river during the warm Nelson summers.

RIWAKA RIVER

■ *Location*
The north branch emerges from an impressive, deep, dark blue spring on the Takaka Hill south of Riwaka township. The main stream flows northeast through farmland and enters Tasman Bay near Riwaka just west of Motueka.

■ *Access*
The scenic Riwaka River Valley road leaves SH 60 a few kilometres west of Riwaka township at the foot of the Takaka Hill and follows up the true left bank. It is a short scramble to the stream. SH 60 crosses the river.

■ *Restrictions*
Artificial bait and fly only. Only one trout longer than 50 cm can be taken. Bag limit is two trout.

This small, clear, shingly stream is overhung by willows and vegetation in places but is a delight to fish and holds good stocks of brown trout in the 0.5–1.2 kg range. Drift dives have revealed good stocks of takeable fish in the river near the Moss Bush picnic area. Use the same flies as for the Motueka River with the addition of a lacemoth pattern. There are some great picnic spots and it's well worth visiting for fly anglers, offering easy access and safe wading though the stones are slippery. Fish are not easy to spot against the brown stones.

MOTUPIKO RIVER

■ *Location*
Drains the St Arnaud Range and flows north to join the Motueka at Kohatu.

■ *Access*

SH 6 follows this river upstream from Kohatu, but a short walk across private farmland is sometimes necessary to reach the river. Public access is available at Quinneys Bush Reserve, Tunnicliffe and Korere bridges. Please note, Quinneys Bush is popular with campers and swimmers in the Christmas holidays.

■ *Restrictions*
Bag limit is two trout, and only artificial bait or fly to be used. Only one fish exceeding 50 cm can be taken.

This is a spawning tributary which joins the Motueka at Kohatu. The river is similar in character to the Motueka but smaller. It tends to fish better early and late in the season as hot summers and reduced water flow often force fish back into the main river.

The best fishing is in the first 5 km above the Motueka confluence. There are only a few fish above this. Fish can easily be spotted, especially in the deeper runs against the cliffs, but just as easily frightened. They respond to the same fly methods used in the parent river. Catch and release is strongly recommended as stocks are not high.

WANGAPEKA RIVER

■ *Location*
Drains the Herbert Range of the Kahurangi National Park, flows in a northerly direction and enters the Motueka River 7 km downstream from Tapawera.

■ *Access*
From Tapawera on SH 61 take the road to Tadmor and Matariki, then follow the Wangapeka River road. This road follows upriver but do not take your vehicle beyond the Dart ford unless the weather is settled or you have a four-wheel-drive. Access to the middle and lower reaches is generally across private farmland but permission is seldom refused a considerate angler.

■ *Restrictions*
Above the Dart confluence, the bag limit is two fish but only one exceeding 50 cm can be taken. Below the Dart ford, four fish can be taken.

The Wangapeka Track follows up this river to the Karamea and Little Wanganui headwaters, a route popular with trampers. In the upper reaches, the banks are bush covered; the middle and lower reaches wind through bracken-covered hills and across farmland. The banks are stable and there are some pleasant pools and runs, but the river discolours easily in a fresh. Fish can be spotted and stalked, especially in the upper reaches, and the brown trout respond in similar fashion to their relatives in the Motueka. To those willing to tramp, fish up to 2.5 kg have been taken in the upper reaches.

The Baton and Pearse tributaries joining the true left bank of the Motueka River near Woodstock used to be favoured 30 years ago, but because of their instability during a fresh, fishing has been patchy. The Pearse gorge is worth exploring. Recent drift dives have revealed a reasonable number of fish in the Baton, especially above the gorge (50 fish/km above the concrete ford). Fish can be spotted in this clear stream draining the Arthur Range.

There are great picnic spots under beech trees in the Baton Valley. Both these tributaries fish better either early or late in the season. The Pearse is reserved for artificial bait and fly fishing and only two fish can be taken.

RAI RIVER
■ *Location and access*
This is a medium-sized tributary of the Pelorus River which joins the main stream at Pelorus Bridge. SH 75, running parallel to this stream for 10 km above the falls in the Rai Valley, provides easy access generally across farmland. Three small feeder streams, the Ronga, Opouri and Tunakino, join the Rai at Carluke.

- *Season*
1 October-30 April

- *Restrictions*
All legal methods can be used in the Rai and the bag limit is four fish. However, in the three small tributaries, the Ronga, Opouri and Tunakino rivers, only artificial bait and fly fishing is permitted and the bag limit is two trout.

This excellent stream flowing across farmland is lined by bush and willows and holds very high stocks of small-to medium-sized brown and rainbow trout (200 fish/km above the falls). These can be spotted in ideal conditions and will accept small nymphs and dry flies carefully presented on fine gear. Trout may be seen scattering in all directions unless one approaches the stream with care. It's not an easy stream to fish because of long, clear glides and bank obstruction, but wading is generally unnecessary except to cross the stream. Fishing is best early in the season as farming effluent and low water flows in summer can cause eutrophication problems. The Rai and its feeder streams are highly recommended to the 'purist' angler.

KARAMEA RIVER
- *Location*
This is by far the largest river in the Kahurangi National Park. The main river rises in the Allen Range where it saddles with the Little Wanganui and Wangapeka rivers. In the first part of its course the river flows north, but at the Leslie junction (Big Bend) it turns to flow west, eventually reaching the Tasman Sea at Karamea township.

- *Access*
• From Karamea: 11 km of the lower reaches can be fished from Arapito or Umere roads. Upstream from here, a track follows the north bank of the river for one and a half hours; then trampers must walk up the riverbed for another three

hours to Greys Hut (six bunks). This route is difficult unless the river is low. It is another day's tramp upriver to the mouth of the Ugly tributary.

• From the Leslie valley: by tramping for five to six hours over the Baton Saddle to the Big Bend. This track can be overgrown and difficult.

• From the Graham valley near Ngatimoti : a two-day tramp over the Mount Arthur tableland.

• From the Trilobite Hut in the Cobb valley via Lake Peel and Balloon Hut on the Mount Arthur tableland.

• From the Wangapeka Track: a two-day walk to Luna Hut at the headwaters of the Karamea. These last two routes are tracked, but tramping experience is advised.

• By helicopter from Nelson or Karamea.

■ *Season*
Downstream from the mouth of the lower gorge, the season is open from 1 October to 30 September, and the bag limit is six trout. Elsewhere, the season is 1 October to 30 April.

■ *Restrictions*
The bag limit is two trout above the cableway in the lower gorge.

The Karamea River and tributaries offer wonderful wilderness brown trout fishing equal to the best in New Zealand. The main river from the Luna Hut all the way to Karamea provides an endless stock of self-sustaining fish averaging around 2 kg.

The upper reaches above the Leslie confluence flow rapidly over a rock and stone bed and offer great nymph, dry and wet fly fishing to the agile boots-and-shorts angler (40 large fish/km have been counted on drift dives above Crow Hut). Fish can be spotted and stalked. The river is quite large by the time it reaches the Leslie junction, but fish can still be spotted and the river forded with care (50 large fish/km at the Bend).

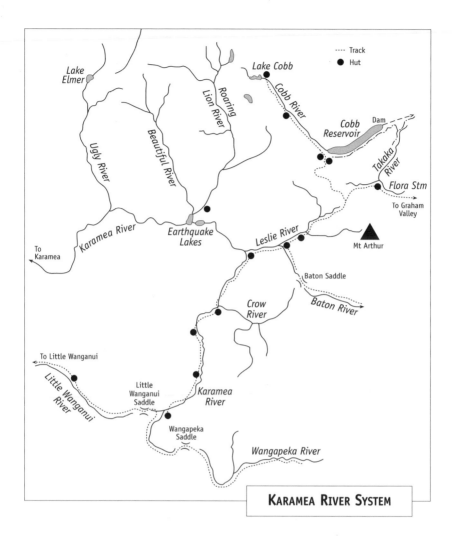

KARAMEA RIVER SYSTEM

Near the Roaring Lion confluence lie the Earthquake Lakes, formed during the Murchison earthquake, and these are well stocked with eels as well as trout. Spinning methods will also enable fish to be taken in all stretches, but especially in the Earthquake Lakes. Below the Roaring Lion, the country becomes very remote and the river gorgy, so angling pressure is minimal, yet there is still superb water.

At Karamea the river is very large, slower flowing and better suited to spinning, but there is an evening rise when conditions are favourable and trout can be taken on a fly.

Drift dives at Arapito reveal good stocks of mainly medium-sized trout (100 fish/km).

KARAMEA TRIBUTARIES

All reasonable-sized tributaries contain fish, but only five will be described.

Crow River

The Crow Hut at the Karamea-Crow junction offers 'back-country accommodation' and a base for fishing this highly rated stream. The river flows in a westerly direction. Fish population is high, but not all are in good condition and poor fish should be returned. The stream is easily waded and best fished in boots and longs for sandfly protection.

This is a typical clear bush stream with a rock and stone river bed where fish can readily be stalked providing you keep out of sight. Fish are not sophisticated feeders and will take a wide range of carefully presented dry flies and nymphs. Try Mole Fly, Coch-y-bondhu, Royal Wulff, Humpy and Deer Hair dry flies or Half Back, Hare and Copper, Perla and Pheasant Tail nymphs in sizes 10–16.

Leslie River

This is the most accessible tributary, and the Leslie Hut or the Karamea Bend Hut on the Karamea offer the best base. It flows south from the Mount Arthur tableland to enter the Karamea River at the Big Bend. For a few years the fishing fell away, but recently the trout have come back. The flies and conditions are the same as for the Crow.

Roaring Lion River

■ *Access*

• A hard day's tramp (five to six hours) down the Karamea river bed from Big Bend. This route is difficult when the river is high, as bush-bashing along the bank becomes necessary.
• From the Cobb Valley either via Kimbell Spur or from Chaffey Hut via Chaffey Stream and Breakfast Creek.

- From the Ugly or Aorere headwaters via Aorere Saddle. Experienced trampers only should tackle these routes.
- Via helicopter to the Roaring Lion Hut.

This is a marvellous river offering similar conditions to the Crow and Leslie, but the river is larger and fords are tricky in the lower reaches, some being more than waist deep. The river flows in a southerly direction through heavily forested, rugged country. Good fishing is available upstream as far as Breakfast Creek. There are trophy fish in this river. Use the same flies as for the Crow. There is a good evening rise, but the sandflies are fierce. Catch and release is strongly recommended.

Beautiful River

This tributary can be easily reached across from the Roaring Lion Hut, providing the Roaring Lion is fordable. Only the lower 2 km is worth fishing, before the river rises steeply and becomes very rough going. There are a few good pools in the first kilometre and trout are easy to spot.

Ugly River

■ *Access*

This is the most remote tributary and only experienced trampers should attempt to reach this valley — either upstream from Karamea, downstream from the Roaring Lion or via the Roaring Lion headwaters.

There is excellent water between McNabb and Domett creeks as well as in the lower reaches where the river is deep and swift. The river flows in a southerly direction from Lake Elmer, formed by a landslide resulting from the Murchison earthquake. The lake itself holds fish, but in our experience they are in poor condition and not worth taking unless you are short of food. Fishing methods and conditions for the Ugly are similar to the other tributaries described. The river holds less water than the Roaring Lion, but it contains the odd trophy fish and clears rapidly after a fresh.

Rafters have negotiated the Karamea River, but the gorge below Kakapo River is rather terrifying.

MOKIHINUI RIVER

■ *Location*

This river drains a very large catchment of rugged bush country, including the Radiant, Allen, Matiri and Lyell Ranges. The north and south branches respectively, flow north and south to the Forks. The main river then flows in a westerly direction to enter the sea at Mokihinui, some 40 km north of Westport.

■ *Access to lower reaches*

• SH 67 and the Mokihinui-Seddonville road provide access to 11 km of the lower reaches. Beyond Seddonville, a four-wheel-drive is advised.

■ *Access to middle reaches*

• From Mokihinui by tramping upstream on a rough track following the south bank of the river. The Forks Hut (sleeps six) is six to eight hours' tramp from the road end. Sinclair Hut (sleeps four) on the north branch is only 30 minutes' walk across the river flats from Forks Hut. There is also a hut on the Johnson River. On the south branch, Goat Creek hut, opposite Hennessy Creek, is three hours' tramp from the Forks and sleeps four.

• By tramping over Kiwi Saddle into the Johnson Tributary from the Wangapeka Track.

• By helicopter from Karamea or Nelson. The fixed wing airstrip at the Forks is at present unserviceable.

■ *Season*

Open all year downstream from the cableway at Welcome Creek. Elsewhere, 1 October to 30 April.

■ *Restrictions*

Above Welcome Creek, the bag limit is two trout.

This is a superb, remote brown trout fishery almost rivalling its northern neighbour, the Karamea, though considerably smaller. There are extensive stretches of clear mountain water with fish averaging 2 kg (30 large fish/km in the north and south branches). This rock-and-stone-type backcountry river winds through dense beech forest and across tussock flats. Trout can be spotted and stalked and respond to a wide selection of dry flies and nymphs. All major tributaries hold fish, the Johnson, Allen, Hemphill, Larrikin and Hennessy creeks being especially recommended. The lower reaches offer sea-run fish to spinners or a smelt fly when the whitebait are running, especially after a fresh. Take insect repellent.

MURCHISON DISTRICT

Murchison is a small country village serving a farming community and lies two hours by car south of Nelson. Scenic attractions include lakes Rotoroa and Rotoiti, the Maruia Falls and the pleasant surrounding countryside shaken up by the Murchison earthquake of 1929. There is an active golf club and the Vault Gallery is worth a visit for handcraft, pottery, jade and paintings. Additional recreational activities include white-water rafting, kayaking, mountain biking, caving, tramping, bush walking, gold panning, jet boating and hunting.

Accommodation is adequate in the mid-town hotels, motels, camping ground, and two luxury lodges situated just out of town. Eating out opportunities are limited.

Major events in the township include a Tree Hugging Festival in February.

There are no fly shops or sports stores but a local professional fly fishing guide has flies for purchase. Additional equipment can be bought in Nelson.

More information can be obtained from:

Information Centre
Waller Street, Murchison
Ph 03 523 9350

NELSON LAKES NATIONAL PARK

The Park covers 100 470 ha of rugged mountains and un-spoiled native bush and contains two major lakes and a number of exciting rivers. Sufficient snow falls in winter to provide skiing on Mount Robert, but summer temperatures warm the lakes for swimming and boating.

Visitors to the park should visit the park headquarters at St Arnaud for maps and general information. There are motel and camping facilities available at both lakes. Insect repellent for sandflies is recommended!

TRAVERS RIVER

■ *Location and access*

Drains Mount Travers (2338 m) and surrounding peaks and flows in a northerly direction down a very scenic valley to enter the head or southern end of Lake Rotoiti. There are well-marked tramping tracks through the bush round both sides of the lake but the journey may take three to four hours. This time can be considerably shortened by hiring a boat to the lakehead or Coldwater huts at the head of the lake.

■ *Restrictions*

Artificial bait and fly; bag limit is two trout, but only one exceeding 50 cm can be taken.

This valley is worth visiting for the scenery alone, as the river winds across wide tussock flats edged with beech bush. The river has a reasonably stable shingle bed and holds brown trout averaging 1 kg which can be stalked in very clear water all the way upstream to the John Tait Hut, but you will be disturbed by trampers in summer. Try Coch-y-bondhu, Royal Wulff, Deer Hair patterns, Irresistible and Adams dry flies, Hare and Copper, Stonefly and Half Back nymphs all in sizes 8–12. The 10 km of fishable water is best fished on hot days from December to March when visibility is good.

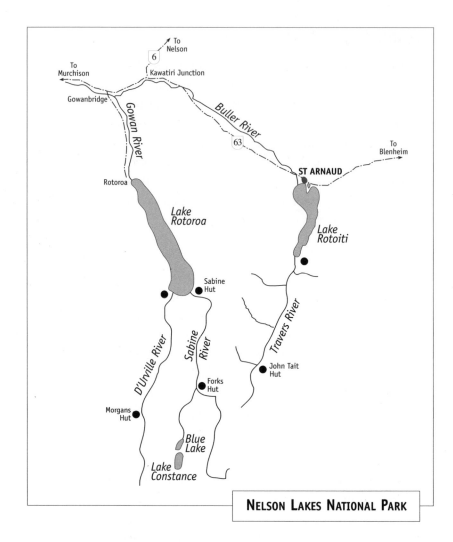

NELSON LAKES NATIONAL PARK

SABINE RIVER

■ *Location*

Drains the Spenser Mountains, Lake Constance (via an underground stream) and the Blue Lake, flows in a north-westerly direction and enters Lake Rotoroa east of the D'Urville mouth.

■ *Access*

By boat from Rotoroa or a five- to six-hour tramp. Check at the ranger station for permission to use the Parks Board huts. A marked track follows upriver to the Sabine Forks Hut about four to five hours' tramp from the head of the lake.

■ *Restrictions*
Artificial bait and fly. Bag limit two fish, only one of which can exceed 50 cm.

This river holds brown and rainbow trout with an occasional fish up to 3 kg. Upstream from the Sabine Hut near the head of the lake there is an unfishable gorge holding a few very large fish. There is good, fishable rock-and-stone mountain stream water all the way to the Forks Hut. Fish can be spotted in the slower pools, but in summer do not neglect the rough, boisterous, well-oxygenated stretches which often hold trout. Lake Constance and the Blue Lake on the west branch are worth a visit for the tramper, but purely for the scenery as they do not hold trout.

D'URVILLE RIVER
■ *Location and access*
D'Urville mouth and D'Urville Hut can be reached by walking round the lake edge from the wharf at Sabine Hut.

■ *Restrictions*
Artificial bait and fly; bag limit two trout, only one of which can exceed 50 cm.

The D'Urville flows in a bush-covered scenic valley parallel to but west of the Sabine. By contrast, this river holds mainly brown trout. Best fished early and late in the season as reduced water flows can force fish back to the lake in dry summer conditions. Trout are easily spotted in bright conditions. There are 12 km of fishable water to well above Morgans Hut. Use the same flies as for the Travers.

BULLER RIVER (UPPER REACHES)

■ *Location*

Drains Lake Rotoiti, flows west to Kawatiri Junction then turns and flows south to Murchison. Below the inaccessible Upper Buller Gorge at Lyell, the river enters the West Coast district.

■ *Access*

SH 6 follows the river upstream from Murchison to Kawatiri Junction; SH 63 follows the river to Lake Rotoiti. There are many access points for anglers off these roads, although a considerable walk across farmland is sometimes needed to reach the river. Below Kawatiri Junction easy access is only available at picnic spots, angler accesses and at the Murchison camping ground.

■ *Restrictions*

Above the Mangles confluence the season ends on 30 April. Below the confluence, there is an open season. Bag limit is four fish below Gowan Bridge but two fish above this bridge.

This highly regarded self-sustaining brown trout fishery holds fish averaging 1.5 kg. Below the confluence with the Gowan, the Buller becomes a large, heavy-water river. The pools and edges of runs should be fished with a large buoyant dry fly or a Stonefly nymph.

The river is stable and flows over a rock-and-stone bed. The stretch upstream from Kawatiri Junction offers excellent fly fishing and fish stocks are good. Fish can be spotted by the observant angler, though many will be missed in the rougher sections of the river. The brown stones provide excellent camouflage for the fish and can be slippery when wading.

In places the river is swift, overgrown and difficult to fish but trout frequent these pockets of rough water and fight vigorously when hooked. During low-water conditions selected fords in the river can be crossed by those wearing boots and shorts, but use a manuka pole for stability.

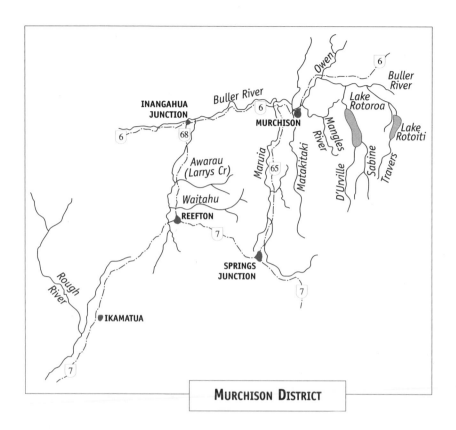

MURCHISON DISTRICT

Trout respond to heavily weighted nymphs such as Hare and Copper, beadhead and Brown Stonefly; in the fast runs use sizes 8–10. A well-hackled dry fly with good flotation features, such as a Yellow Humpy, Irresistible, Stimulator or Royal Wulff in sizes 8–12, is equally well accepted.

The upper reaches remain clear even after a fresh. Around Murchison there is often a vigorous sedge rise on warm summer evenings. Try a Deer Hair Sedge or small wet fly on a floating line fished across and down.

Two tributaries of the upper Buller are worth exploring early in the season. The Howard River enters the true left bank while Station Creek enters the true right bank. There is road access to both streams from SH 63.

OWEN RIVER

■ *Location and access*

This small, gentle stream flows in a southerly direction from the Lookout Range and Mount Owen to join the Buller at Owen River Junction on SH 6 a few kilometres south of Gowanbridge. The Owen Valley road follows the river upstream for 12 km on the true left bank, but access to the river is difficult in places due to blackberry, scrub, bracken and willows. The river bed is easy to negotiate. There are a few marked anglers' access tracks.

■ *Restrictions*

Artificial bait and fly; bag limit two trout only one of which exceeds 50 cm.

Owen River

The Owen is a delightful stream to fish. The water is slightly greenish in colour but brown trout up to 3 kg can be spotted in bright conditions. The river is easy to wade and cross but the stones can be slippery. Patches of beech bush along the banks enhance the scenic qualities of this stream which is best fished early in the season. Fish become very wary later in the season as this is a very popular river. Catch and release recommended.

MANGLES RIVER

■ *Location*
Rises in the bush-clad Braeburn range. The Te Wiriki, Tiraumea and Tutaki tributaries join at Tutaki to form the Mangles while the Blackwater joins lower down. This small river flows in a westerly direction to join the Buller at Longford a few kilometres north of Murchison on SH 6.

■ *Access*
The Tutaki Valley road leaves SH 6 about 5 km north of Murchison at Longford and follows the river to Tutaki.

■ *Restrictions*
Artificial bait and fly; bag limit two trout.

This delightful medium-sized stream holds good stocks of brown trout averaging 1 kg (130 fish/km in the gorge), and is highly recommended. Fish are not easy to spot in the lower reaches or gorge where the river is overgrown in places with beech bush, scrub and blackberry, and the water is boisterous and clear, brownish in colour. There are also some very deep holes. We suggest fishing through the gorge in low-water summer conditions only. However, 10 km upstream, the river flows across farmland and is more sedate with well-developed pools and riffles.

Fish respond to most weighted nymphs in sizes 12–16. There's often a good evening rise on this stream but watch for fish taking emergers and breaking the surface rather than rising. The river can be waded, even through the gorge in

Mangles River

low-water summer conditions, but the river bed is very slippery. Fishes best early in the season as fish become shy in low water after being fished over by other anglers. Catch and release is recommended. Please ask for permission to cross private farmland.

The Tutaki and Te Wiriki tributaries hold some good fish, especially early and late in the season. There is road access to both streams.

MATAKITAKI RIVER

■ *Location and access*

Drains the Spenser Mountains and generally follows a northwesterly course to join the Buller just south of Murchison. The road to Matakitaki and Upper Matakitaki from Murchison generally follows up the river although at times it is some distance away across private land. The upper reaches can be reached via the Mangles — Tutaki Valley road through Tutaki to the Matakitaki Station. Permission should be obtained before tramping up the valley.

■ *Restrictions*

There is an open season only below SH 6 and the bag limit is four fish. Above SH 6 the bag limit is two fish.

There are only a few fish in deep pools in the headwaters around Downie Hut. Below this point and as far downstream as Upper Matakitaki, the river tends to be large, shingly and unstable during floods. At Matakitaki, the river is more confined and flows through beech bush and farmland with an occasional gorgy stretch. It holds brown trout in the 1–1.5 kg range although there is always the chance of a larger fish. The braided section is more suited to spinning but there are stretches of good nymph water in the more stable sections. The lower reaches are often silt laden from a tributary entering the west bank of the main river so do not be discouraged by the appearance of the river at the main road bridge on SH 6 on the outskirts of Murchison. Floods in recent seasons have depleted the fish stocks but the parent Buller River rapidly restocks this river.

There are some small side creeks worth fishing early and late in the season. Six Mile, Station and Nardoo creeks can all hold fish.

The Glenroy tributary, reached from the Glenroy Valley road, holds few fish. The river is flood-prone, fast flowing, unstable and may carry snow melt even as late as December.

MARUIA RIVER

■ *Location and access*

Rises in the Spenser Mountains and flows in a southerly direction through Cannibal Gorge to meet SH 7 at Maruia Springs in the Lewis Pass. Follows SH 7 to Springs Junction then turns northwest and follows SH 65 and the Shenandoah Road to join the Buller River 10 km southwest of Murchison. Access is not difficult from SH 65 and from a number of side roads.

■ *Restrictions*

Bag limit is four fish below the Maruia Falls but two fish only above the falls.

This moderate-sized river is highly recommended and holds good stocks of medium to large fish in clear mountain water flowing over a shingle and rock bed (drift dive figures reveal 100 fish/km at Paenga). Above the Maruia Falls the banks are lined with beech bush and clumps of manuka, while the lower reaches flow through willows. Below the Maruia Falls, formed during the Murchison earthquake, there are only brown trout, while above the Falls there are both rainbow and brown with the latter predominating.

There are only a few fish in the braided unstable water above the Woolley confluence but some are large. The best water is in the gorge west of Mount Rutland where the river leaves the road between Ruffe Creek and the Warwick Stream confluence. However, it takes a very long day's tramp to negotiate the entire gorge.

For less energetic anglers there is excellent water upstream from West Bank Bridge, at Peasoup Creek, Creighton Road and at Boundary Creek. Fish can be spotted and stalked with dry fly or nymph in the smaller sizes but a careful approach and a long leader is essential for success. The river takes some time to clear after heavy rain. There is also excellent spinning water in a number of spots, especially where fly casting is impossible.

WAITAHU RIVER

■ *Location and access*

This major tributary of the Inangahua River drains the Victoria Range and flows on a northwesterly course to enter the Inangahua 5 km northwest of Reefton. It is one hour's drive from Murchison to Reefton. Gannons Road from SH 69 leads to and crosses the river. From here a very rough four-wheel-drive and walking track leads upstream on the true right bank as far as the Montgomerie River confluence, but it is safer to leave your vehicle near the settling ponds situated on the true left bank and walk from there.

■ *Season*

1 October-30 April

■ *Restrictions*

Bag limit is two trout.

This is a pleasant, clear, greenish-coloured scenic river holding some good-sized browns in clear pools and runs to well beyond the confluence of the Waitahu and Montgomerie rivers. Fish numbers are not high and present quite a challenge during low water flows in summer, but an angler with a cautious approach and fine gear should see results. The river has been polluted by coalmines from time to time and is quite heavily fished and poached by the locals. Although plenty of walking is required, the Montgomerie tributary is well worth fishing. Try Coch-y-bondhu, Deer Hair, Humpy, Stimulator and Royal Wulff dry flies or Hare and Copper, Caddis, Stonefly, Half Back and Pheasant Tail nymphs, all in sizes 14–18. Use a long trace and be careful not to line the fish. There are 10 km of good water and the nor'wester tends to blow up the valley.

AWARAU RIVER (LARRYS CREEK)

■ *Location and access*

Flows through bush country on a parallel course north of the

Waitahu and joins the Inangahua 14 km northwest of Reefton on SH 69. Access to the lower reaches is from the picnic area or SH 69 bridge. Access to the middle and upper reaches is on foot from the end of the forestry road up the true right bank.

■ *Restrictions*
Bag limit is two trout, catch and release is recommended.

Another boots-and-shorts stream, the Awarau is similar to the Waitahu. It has a reputation for the occasional large fish (up to 4.5 kg), especially early in the season. However, these fish have grown to this size for a very good reason. They are wily and cunning! Many pools and runs are deep and swift and fish are very difficult to spot except on a bright day. It is also difficult to fish deep enough with a small nymph and land fish on light tippet material. Two days and a campout are required in order to fish this river adequately. It has become very popular and reputable over recent years along with the Caledonia pool. Overseas anglers are advised to hire a guide if intending to fish this river.

ROUGH RIVER (OTUTUTU)

■ *Location and access*
Rises on the eastern side of the Paparoa Range and flows for 30 km on a southeasterly course to join the Grey at Ikamatua. It is 1 hour 45 minutes' drive from Murchison to Ikamatua. Access to the lower reaches from Ikamatua on the Atarau Road. For the upper reaches, take Mirfins Road where it leaves Atarau Road and follows up the true left bank; turn left through the sawmill. The sawmill gates close at the end of each working day and at weekends. Anglers need to tramp the river to reach the best fishing. This valley has no tracks or huts, but there is cleared farmland to the Mirfin confluence. It is a long day's fishing from the sawmill to Mirfin Creek and back. Many anglers fly in by helicopter. Overseas visitors should procure the services of a guide.

■ *Season*

1 October-30 April.

■ *Restrictions*

Bag limit is two trout.

The Rough is a very popular, boisterous, bouldery, rock-and-stone river flowing through native bush and holding fish up to 4.5 kg. Trout can be spotted in crystal-clear, greenish water, but many will be missed in the rough white water, and they must be approached with caution and skill. It is a boots-and-shorts stream for the adventurous and fit, with over 15 km of fishable water to well above the Gordon Creek confluence, the best fishing being upstream from Mirfin Creek. The river can be forded at the tail of most pools and the rocks are not very slippery.

Guides bring paying clients to this river and many fly in by helicopter. A friend did just that a couple of years ago but encountered torrential rain for four days and was glad to be flown out without wetting his line in the river. Such is fishing on the West Coast! Catch and release is recommended.

LAKE BRUNNER
DISTRICT

Lake Brunner and the small settlement of Moana lie in the Central West Coast of the South Island, a 45 minute drive from Greymouth, the main town. On a fine sunny day there is no better place to be on earth than the West Coast. Unfortunately, fine sunny days are few except during February and March as the precipitation annually can be as high as 3500 mm in this area. Despite wet weather and the sandflies, the scenery is breathtaking and the brown trout fishing superb.

Aside from the angling and scenery, the West Coast offers other fascinating diversions as well. One should visit Shantytown and pan for gold, browse through craft shops and jade galleries, and best of all, wash down a few beers with the locals in a country pub. Your itinerary should also include the Putai Blow Hole and Pancake Rocks at Punakaiki and a drive to South Westland to view Franz Josef and Fox glaciers. A scenic drive over Haast Pass to Wanaka might also be included. In summer, bird watchers must visit the white heron colony near Okarito from Whataroa.

Scheduled bus services operate from Nelson, Picton and Christchurch and the Trans Alpine Express from Christchurch to Greymouth via Moana is one of the world's finest train journeys. All three routes to the coast by car are stunning; from Nelson via the Buller Gorge; from Christchurch via the Lewis Pass or Arthur's Pass.

Accommodation is simple but comfortable on the Coast with hotels, motels, lodges, farmstays, camping grounds and cabins. There are no luxury hotels but a few of the local restaurants may surprise you.

The West Coast Wine and Food Festival should not be overlooked as local fare may include whitebait, wild pork, venison, possum, huhu grubs and other regional 'delicacies'.

There are sports stores in Westport, Greymouth and Hokitika but fly fishing merchandise may be limited. Professional guides are available for hire.

More information can be obtained from:
West Coast Tourism Council
PO Box 65, Greymouth
Ph 03 768 0466

HAUPIRI RIVER

■ *Location and access*

There are two branches to this river. The clear water rain- and snow-fed branch rises close to the Harper Pass, then follows a northwesterly direction flowing through bush-clad mountains before joining the other heavily peat-stained branch draining Lake Haupiri. Gradually the clear and brown waters mingle in the main river which enters the Ahaura at Haupiri. Take the Nelson Creek-Kopara Road to the Haupiri School. The private Wallace Road follows the clear tributary upstream. It is a 40 minute drive from Moana. Permission is required. The main river is crossed just before the school. Access is not difficult to this section below the tributary confluence although the river flows some distance from the road.

■ *Season*

1 October-30 April.

■ *Restrictions*

Upstream from the confluence with the lake outlet, the bag limit is two trout only.

Across the farmland, the clearwater branch has been modified by stop banks; however, there are still some good

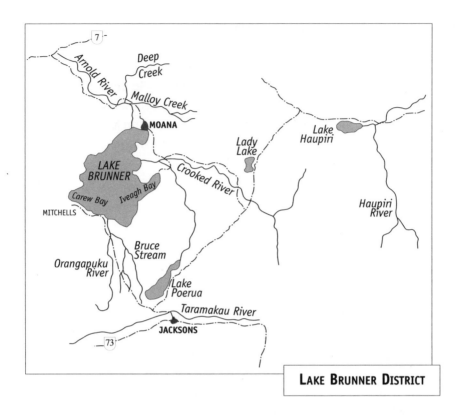

LAKE BRUNNER DISTRICT

brown trout in well-defined pools and runs. Upstream from the farm, there is excellent water for fly fishing, and fish up to 4 kg are easily spotted in large pools as far up as the hot springs (8 km above the farm). This is boots-and-shorts fishing with plenty of walking required in a backcountry rock-and-stone river. We recommend catch and release in this section of river. The confluence of these two branches lies just upstream from the road bridge and can be reached from an obscure bush track 0.5 km upstream from the bridge. Fish stocks are very high in this section of water (200 fish/km). Trout can be seen lying along the line where the clear and brown lake waters mingle. A small overgrown side creek, Clear Stream, enters just above this confluence and always holds a few fish in gin-clear, still water. These present a real challenge. Downstream from the road bridge the river becomes quite large, flowing over a shingle bed and across

Exploring a West Coast stream

farmland, and it holds a good stock of browns in the 1–2 kg range. These can be caught on flies and spinners.

ARNOLD RIVER

■ *Location*
Drains Lake Brunner at Moana and flows in a northerly direction to enter the Grey River at Stillwater on SH 7 about 10 km from Greymouth. There is a hydro-electric dam 13 km below Lake Brunner at Kaimata and the water which backs up for 4 km is known as Lake Ullstrom.

■ *Access*
From Arnold Valley Road to Lake Brunner at Stillwater, Kokiri Bridge, Arnold River bridge at Aratika, Kotuku and the lake outlet. There is good water off Blairs Block Road to Kohatu. Turn off and cross the river at the meat processing works.

■ *Season*

Open all year. Bag limit is six trout.

This fast-flowing, medium-sized, tea-coloured tributary of the Grey, holding numerous brown and the occasional rainbow trout averaging 1–2 kg, is highly regarded and heavily fished although access is rather limited. The banks are covered in places by native bush and in other stretches by willows. Most fishing is done on the lower 11 km below the dam, but drift dives have also revealed high numbers of fish above the dam at Kotuku (240 fish/km) and at Kokiri (75 fish/km).

The river is stable and seldom floods but can become discoloured for two or three days after heavy rain from silt-laden water entering from Malloy and Deep creeks. It is very difficult to fish when Lake Brunner is high. Fish cannot be spotted, as they often lie deep and the stones are slippery to wade.

The insect life is prolific. Try a well-weighted nymph on a sink-tipped line and a long trace, a small wet March Brown or Twilight Beauty on a sinking line or a well-hackled dry fly such as Royal Wulff, Coch-y-bondhu or a Deer Hair pattern on a floating line. At times, a green beetle imitation can be deadly. In the evening, fish will rise to a Twilight Beauty and accept a Deer Hair sedge fished across and down. Fish can also be taken on a spinner or a night lure such as Mrs Simpson and Hairy Dog fished on a sinking line. Do not ignore rough water as many fish lie in pockets and along the edges.

Two small tea-coloured streams, Deep Creek and the Malloy Creek, join the Arnold at Kotuku north of Moana. Both hold fish and are well worth investigating, especially in low-water conditions. Deep Creek often has a thin oil slick on the surface as a natural seepage has been occurring for many years. The Arnold Valley Road crosses both creeks near the Kotuku rail station.

LAKE BRUNNER

■ *Season*

Open all year.

■ *Restrictions*

From 1 May to 30 September fishing is not permitted within 100 m of any inflowing tributary. Bag limit is six trout.

■ *Boat launching facilities*

At Moana, Iveagh Bay and Mitchells.

At 10 km across this is the largest lake. Most of the shoreline is covered in native bush. Deep trolling accounts for most fish although the outlet is a hot spot for live-bait fishing after dark. There is good trolling water from Howitt Point through to Swan Bay, with the Crooked Delta (Howitt Point), Hohonu Delta (Hohonu Spit) and the Orangapuku Delta (Swan Bay) especially good late in the season when fish are gathering for their spawning runs. Spinners, such as varieties of Toby and Cobra and Tasmanian Devil, take most fish.

For the shoreline angler, try Iveagh Bay, Swan Bay, and Carew Bay through to the Hohonu Delta, providing the lake level is not too high. Although the water is peat-stained from native bush run-off, trout can be spotted in bright, still conditions and will accept Hare and Copper, Pheasant Tail and damsel nymphs, and lures such as Hairy Dog, Hamill's Killer, Mrs Simpson or Fuzzywuzzy. Fly casting from a boat is good at the mouth of the Orangapuku and Bruce rivers. The trout population is very high.

LAKE POERUA

■ *Season*

Starts on 1 October and ends on 30 April.

■ *Restrictions*

Bag limit is six trout.

■ *Boat launching facilities*

At Te Kinga Reserve.

This lake holds mainly brown trout and a few rainbow trout, and these fish have a very orange flesh from eating koura (freshwater crayfish). Sockeye salmon were released into this lake in 1984 but have not thrived. Most fish are caught by trolling. There is some shoreline fly fishing along the eastern and swampy southern shore in November–December before the shallow lake becomes weedy. A damsel fly nymph or Hamill's Killer fished on a floating line can be very effective. The lake is peat-coloured but fish can be spotted in the shallows in bright conditions. Casting a large Greenwell's Glory or Royal Wulff dry fly from a drifting boat along the bush-covered western shore can bring results.

ORANGIPUKU RIVER

■ *Location and access*
This stream flows almost from the Taramakau River valley round the base of the Hohonu Range and joins Bruce Creek just prior to entering Swan Bay at the southern end of Lake Brunner. The Kumara-Inchbonnie Road crosses the lower reaches of the Orangipuku. A farm track follows down the true right bank almost to the mouth from this bridge.

■ *Season*
1 October–30 April

■ *Boat launching facilities*
Only the lower 3 km of the Orangipuku is worth fishing, as water flows above this level can be unreliable. There are a few good pools above the bridge. This is a clearwater stream where fish can easily be spotted. The river is shingly and rapidly becomes unfishable after heavy rain, as the head-waters flow through cleared farmland. The banks are lined by patches of willow, native bush, blackberry and gorse. Stocks can vary within a few days; at times plenty of fish move into the river from the lake while at other times trout seem to return to the larger water. Fishing is often best late in the season when a spawning run of browns occurs.

BRUCE CREEK

■ *Location and access*

Drains swampy land near the southern end of Lake Poerua, skirts the base of Mount Te Kinga and joins the Orangipuku upstream from Swan Bay. Take the northernmost side road, 1 km east of the Orangipuku bridge, off the Kumara-Inchbonnie Road. This runs toward Mount Te Kinga and crosses the stream at an old farm bridge. It pays to seek permission from the landowner, but this is seldom refused.

■ *Season*

1 October–30 April

This is an entirely different stream from the Orangipuku, being spring-fed and remaining clear after rain. There are some deep holes and fast-flowing runs, but generally the stream flows quite placidly across farmland. The water is a weak tea colour, the stone river bed brownish and weedy. Fish can sometimes be spotted in bright conditions. Stocks of brown trout are higher than they appear, as fish often remain hidden during the day under long strands of green weed.

There is sometimes an evening rise on warm summer evenings. Trout then appear in great numbers and feed voraciously. Fish, which average 1.3 kg with an occasional one up to 2.5 kg, can be taken by skilful fly anglers, but catch and release is recommended. About 1 km upstream from the farm bridge, the stream divides into three. The middle tributary offers a further 1 km of challenging water where fish can be more easily spotted on patches of sandy river bed. Use small dry flies and weighted nymphs on a long trace. During the evening rise, try a CDC or Elk Hair Caddis. If this fails, switch to a small emerger pattern. This stream is strongly recommended to the purist. Fish numbers are high but they are not easily brought to the net.

South Island trophy rainbow

CROOKED RIVER

■ *Location and access*

Drains the Alexander Range and flows in a northeasterly direction to enter the eastern side of Lake Brunner south of Howitt Point. It is 11 km by road south from Moana to Te Kinga where the river is first reached. The road to Iveagh Bay crosses near the mouth. The road from Te Kinga to Rotomanu follows the river upstream and crosses the river south of Rotomanu. The Bell Hill-Inchbonnie Road crosses higher upstream at the Crooked River Reserve. A rough private farm road follows upstream on the true left bank to the confluence of the Evans River tributary and then follows this river for a further 6 km. Permission must be obtained from the landowner.

■ *Season*
1 October–30 April

Quite a large river in the lower reaches, which is best fished from a boat, there is excellent clear fly water across private farmland in the vicinity of Rotomanu and upstream as far as the Bell Hill-Inchbonnie Road bridge. There are well-defined pools and runs. The river is safe to wade, as the river bed is shingle and is not slimy — frequent floods remove any algal covering. Fish stocks can be unreliable, but generally brown trout in the 1–2.4 kg range offer plenty of sport for fly and spin anglers. Fish can be spotted when the river is low and clear. The river gorges above the Bell Hill-Inchbonnie bridge. Upstream from the gorge to just above the Evans River junction and the farm bridge there is a limited amount of fishing water. Fish can sometimes be spotted in the pocket water along the edges of pools, but do not neglect fishing some of the fast water blind with a good flotation dry fly or heavily weighted nymph. Results can be surprising.

The Evans River is a major spawning stream for Lake Brunner but is unstable, fast-flowing and has no holding water. It is not worth fishing.

Above the Evans tributary, the Crooked River enters a second gorge. There is good fishing above the gorge for experienced tramper-anglers.

OMARAMA DISTRICT

Omarama is a small country town in North Otago nestled on the barren tussock plains of the Mackenzie country. It is the centre of gliding in New Zealand and the world championships were held there in 1995. In summer the weather is generally dry and warm but the wind can be problematic at times. Nearby Lake Ruataniwha is a world-class rowing venue and is one of a number of lakes created when the Upper Waitaki River was harnessed for hydro-electric power. Lake Benmore is the largest of these lakes to be formed.

The surrounding countryside although rather bleak has great scenic appeal and Mount Cook National Park is only a two-hour drive away. In early December this drive is spectacular because the roadside lupins are in full bloom. Glacial flour in lakes Pukaki and Tekapo enhance their colour and beauty and the view through the altar window from the Church of the Good Shepherd at Tekapo has been photographed many times over. If time and weather permit a flight from the Hermitage onto the Tasman Glacier by ski plane should not be missed.

Accommodation in Omarama includes hotels, motels and a motor camp but restaurant facilities are minimal.

A small fly shop is attached to one of the motels but anglers would be wise to stock up in Christchurch. A couple working from their home in Twizel (a 30-minute drive north on SH 8) tie flies for purchase. Professional trout fishing guides are available for hire for lake fishing on Benmore and fly fishing the surrounding streams and rivers.

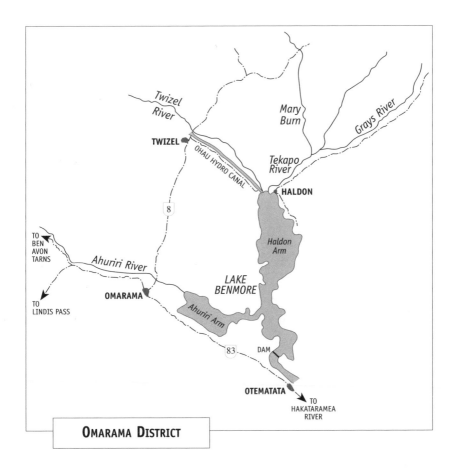

OMARAMA DISTRICT

More information on the Mackenzie country can be obtained from:

Visitor Information
PO Box 522, Timaru
Ph 03 688 0163
Fax 03 688 6162

HAKATARAMEA RIVER

■ *Location*

Rises in the Mackenzie country south of Fairlie and flows on a southerly course to join the Waitaki River at Hakataramea on the opposite bank to Kurow. It is an hour's drive from Omarama.

■ *Access*
Hakataramea Valley and McHenrys roads follow up both sides of the river from Hakataramea.

■ *Season*
1 October–30 April

■ *Restrictions*
Fly fishing only. Bag limit is four fish.

This favoured salmon-spawning stream was subjected to severe flooding in 1985 followed by a drought. It has since recovered and holds good stocks of brown and rainbow trout which can at times be spotted and fished for with dry flies or nymphs.

In the lower reaches, trout tend to be smaller but plentiful (140 small and medium-sized fish/km). Higher upstream in the gorge, trout are less plentiful but larger. Early in the season there are 30 km of fishable water, but fish tend to drop back downstream from the upper reaches during summer low-water conditions. A very popular small stream with easy access, it has a rock-and-shingle bed and is fringed with willows.

LAKE BENMORE
■ *Location*
Lies in the Mackenzie country between Twizel, Omarama and Otematata. Boat ramps are located at Sailors Cutting on Ahuriri Arm and off Grays Road at the Haldon Boat Harbour. There are excellent camping facilities at both these locations.

■ *Access*
• Turn off SH 8 at Dog Kennel Corner near Burke Pass and take the Haldon road to the east side of Haldon Arm.
• The Tekapo Canal road (leaves SH 8 opposite the road to Lake Alexandrina) and its extension, the Ministry of Works Tekapo-Pukaki River road, follow the true right bank of the

Stream mouth, high country lake

Tekapo River from the Tekapo Power House to Haldon Arm. This is a rough, dry-weather road as there are unbridged fords. There is a bridge — the Iron Bridge — across the lower Tekapo River.

• From Ruataniwha Dam, the Falstone Road leads to the west side of Haldon Arm.

• From the Ohau B Power Station, the canal road leads to the lake and the Ohau River mouth.

• From SH 83, drive to the Benmore Dam and Ahuriri delta.

■ *Season*
This lake is open all year round. Bag limit is four fish.

Formed in 1964, this lake has 116 km of rather inaccessible shoreline. There are two arms to the lake: Haldon Arm with its somewhat milky glacial water from the Tasman Glacier and from spillway discharges; and Ahuriri Arm with clear, snow-fed river water. The lake holds vast stocks of brown and rainbow trout and a few landlocked sockeye salmon.

Most fish are taken by deep trolling from boats using lead lines or by live-bait fishing with worms, but cruising fish can be spotted in the shallower bays in favourable summer conditions, especially when the lake is not too high. Trout average 0.75–1.5 kg.

The Ahuriri mouth and delta is very popular for fly fishing. During the day, cruising fish can be stalked and cast to in the shallows along the edges of the tussock shore, in the deep channels and over the weed beds with a small, lightly weighted nymph, Midge Pupa, Corixa, wet fly or dry fly of the Coch-y-bondhu, Royal Wulff or Irresistible varieties. However, keep low and out of sight of cruising fish as they tend to be very wary.

The lake level will often determine the catch rate in this area. If it is flat calm, then cast onto a sandy patch and activate the fly when a fish approaches. Casting at fish in these clear conditions will only scare them off.

Winter fishing is quite popular in this lake, and good catches are made deep trolling from boats even when the surrounding countryside is covered with snow. Suggest survival gear is worn during these conditions!

AHURIRI RIVER

■ *Location*

Rises in the Southern Alps below Mount Huxley and between lakes Ohau and Hawea. Flows on a curving easterly course to enter Lake Benmore near Omarama.

■ *Access*

The delta is described under Lake Benmore, and there's an anglers' access off SH 83. Although some distance away, SH 8 runs parallel to the river from Omarama to Dunstan Downs Station. There is access to the true left bank from the Quail Burn road and the turn-off to Clay Cliffs. A metalled road to Birchwood and Ben Avon stations follows up the river for 25 km from where SH 8 turns south towards the Lindis Pass. It is a relatively short walk across to the river from this road.

Upper Ahuriri River

Permission should be obtained from Ben Avon and Birchwood stations before crossing private land to fish.

■ *Season*
1 November to 30 April. Above Longslip Creek and in the east branch, first Saturday in December to 30 April.

■ *Restrictions*
The bag limit below Longslip Creek is four fish; above Longslip and in the east branch, two fish. No live-bait fishing is permitted.

This medium to large river has a high reputation, and deservedly so. The middle and lower reaches are willow-lined, braided, shingly and unstable and flow across exposed tussock flats, but they still hold good stocks of brown and rainbow in the 1–1.5 kg range (90 fish/km), especially in the stretch from SH 8 bridge to the lake. Most fish are taken from this area on spinners or lures fished across and down, but there's also excellent nymph and dry fly fishing. Downstream lure fishing tends to attract smaller fish and these should be carefully returned.

There's good water higher upstream in the vicinity of the Clay Cliffs but recent floods have changed the river and filled pools with shingle; however, good-sized browns and rainbows can be taken from these braided waters on a well-weighted nymph or a buoyant dry fly. Fish are not easy to spot in this section.

The ox-bows and Maori Cutting on Ben Avon Station offer excellent weighted nymph and terrestrial dry fly fishing. There are some large fish in this area so 3 kg tippets should be used. Some fish are difficult to spot but rise readily to a Cicada pattern cast close to the bank. The river can be crossed in summer low-water conditions but snow melt can persist until Christmas in some years.

The clear pools and runs in upper reaches above Birchwood Station hold only a few fish (two fish/km on drift dives) up to 4.5 kg. These are mainly cunning browns, whose x-ray vision poses a real challenge. The nor'wester whistles down this valley so make the most of an upstream breeze! By 10 am the wind invariably blows down the valley. The mountain views upstream compensate to some extent for the prevailing wind. The river bed provides one of the last habitats for the endangered black stilt.

Ben Avon, Horseshoe, Watson, Green and Yellow lagoons (Ahuriri Valley lagoons)

■ *Location and access*
These lagoons are accessible off the Ben Avon-Birchwood road on private land 2 km north of Ben Avon Station. The lagoons formed from the original Ahuriri river bed lie between the road and the Ahuriri River. Permission should be obtained from Ben Avon Station.

■ *Season*
First Saturday in December to 30 April.

■ *Restrictions*
Fly fishing only.

These waters contain large browns which cruise in tantalising fashion off weed beds. They do not seem to be interested in dry flies but will take a nymph, provided you can keep it out of the weeds. Use a size 14 unweighted Pheasant Tail, Dragon fly or Damsel nymph, or a Cicada imitation on hot summer days. If you hook a fish and land it you can be well satisfied. Like most lake-living browns these fish have a regular beat and are so predictable they can be timed. Woe betide any fish that stray onto foreign territory — they are quickly chased away by the occupier!

The shore is swampy with a few willows. When the Ahuriri River floods, the river can flow through these lagoons which may become lightly silt-laden. The private lagoon lying on the left-hand side of the road just before the turn-off to Ben Avon also holds a few large browns but the water is peat-stained and spotting is impossible.

GRAYS RIVER

■ *Location and access*

Drains swampy country near Burke Pass, flows south and joins the Tekapo River. Haldon Road turns off SH 8 at Dog Kennel Corner, west of Burke Pass, to the Haldon Arm of Lake Benmore and follows the true left bank, albeit some distance away across farmland. There are rough four-wheel-drive tracks across private farmland to the river off this road. A rough metalled road from the Iron Bridge over the Tekapo River upstream from Haldon camping ground follows the true left bank of the Tekapo River to the Grays River confluence. Four-wheel-drive vehicles are safer on these roads, as there are some fords, which although negotiable in dry weather, become difficult after rain.

■ *Season*

1 November to 30 April.

Grays River holds a good stock of trout, a few rainbow in the lower reaches, and browns. There are 10 km of fishable water upstream from the Tekapo confluence. The lower reaches are choked by willows, but upstream beyond these there is excellent fishing in clear water. The river has a shingle, sand-and-weed bed and grassy, willow-lined banks. The middle and upper reaches resemble a chalk stream. The river tends to dry somewhat over a long hot summer but will still hold resident fish.

TEKAPO RIVER

■ *Location*
Drains Lake Tekapo and flows south to enter Haldon Arm on Lake Benmore. The Tekapo-Pukaki Canal road leaves SH 8 opposite the Glenmore-Godley Peaks road and follows down the true right bank, finally crossing the lower reaches at the Iron Bridge above Haldon Arm. A rough metalled road follows up the true left bank from Haldon Arm to the Grays River confluence. A sealed road leaves SH 8 at Ohau B Power Station, following the canal to Lake Benmore and the mouth. The lower reaches of the Ohau River can then be forded in a four-wheel-drive vehicle and a rough metalled road leads upstream on the true right bank of the Tekapo River.

■ *Season*
1 November to 30 April. Below the powerlines, the river is open all year.

This medium-sized river is subject to fluctuating flow rates as a result of hydro-electric power generation. Despite this, the river holds enormous stocks of trout (250 fish/km on drift dives) and is highly recommended in favourable conditions. The upper reaches are often virtually dry due to hydro-electric power modification, and the river only becomes worthwhile below the Forks Stream confluence. The best fishing water lies between the mouth and the Mary Burn confluence in the Grays Hills area. The Tekapo flows down a wide, exposed, barren, shingle river bed with occasional clumps of willow lining the banks. There are well-developed deep pools and long glides, which are easy to fish on still days. The river holds mainly browns with some very large fish lying at the head of deep holes. These should be fished with well-weighted nymphs during the day or a mouse imitation at night. There is a good rise on calm evenings. The river easily becomes unfishable after rain, due mainly to silt being brought down by the Forks Stream. In the lower reaches there are a number of side channels and ponds, all of which hold trout.

TWIZEL RIVER

■ *Location and access*
Drains the Ben Ohau Range, flows on a southerly course through the outskirts of Twizel township and eventually enters the Haldon Arm of Lake Benmore. Crossed by SH 8 near Twizel. A private farm road follows down the true right bank and there is access to the lower reaches after crossing the Ohau River mouth. Access to the upper reaches is from SH 8 and Rhoboro Station Road.

■ *Season*
1 November to 30 April.

■ *Restrictions*
Bag limit is two fish.

This river has a shingle bed and is willow-lined in parts with well-developed pools and runs. It holds a good stock of mainly brown trout that can be spotted in clear conditions. Effluent from Twizel township was thought to have polluted this river, but we found this a pleasant and worthwhile river to fish, especially downstream from SH 8. There is also good water above SH 8 with brown trout in the 0.75–1.2 kg range.

MARY BURN

■ *Location and access*
Flows on a southerly course parallel to the eastern shoreline of Lake Pukaki, is crossed by SH 8 and eventually joins the

Side pressure on a strong fish

Tekapo River in the Grays Hills area after crossing Mackenzie country farmland. The Tekapo-Pukaki Canal road crosses the lower reaches just above the Tekapo River confluence. There's a pleasant campsite near this ford under the willows and silver birches.

■ *Season*
1 November to 30 April.

Mary Burn is a small clear stream flowing across the barren and exposed Mackenzie plain. It should only be fished on a bright, calm day allowing fish to be spotted and stalked. The nor'wester prohibits upstream fly fishing even though the banks of low tussock do not impede casting. Both brown and rainbow up to 3 kg respond to dry flies and nymphs and in ideal weather conditions, the fishing can be exciting. On dull, windy days you will be hard pressed to spot a fish and they are easily spooked by blind casting. Most fish lie in small pools created by this meandering stream and the most productive stretch lies in the region of the power pylons.

WANAKA DISTRICT

The small holiday and retirement township of Wanaka lies on the shores of beautiful Lake Wanaka in West Otago. If you are in pursuit of outdoor activities this is a haven, as hunting, aerobatic and scenic flights, guided tramping, horse trekking, jet boating, kayaking, mountaineering, paragliding, rock climbing and rafting are all available. In winter, there are a number of challenging skifields close by.

Other interesting features include the New Zealand Warbirds Museum, the Wanaka Air Show, photographic tours, four-wheel-drive tours, an enormous human maze and wine tasting at Rippon Vineyard. The town also offers two small local galleries, a library, a golf course and many picnic and barbecue areas.

There is a wide choice of accommodation including camping ground and motorhome sites, cabins, backpackers, bed and breakfasts, homestays, farmstays, motels, hotels and resorts. Some interesting cafes and restaurants add to the local flavour. It is approximately six hours' drive from Christchurch and four and a half hours from Dunedin.

You would be wise to fill your fly boxes in Christchurch or Dunedin although some fishing gear can be purchased in the township. A number of professional fishing guides are available for fly fishing or boat fishing on the lakes.

For more information contact:
Wanaka Promotion Association
PO Box 147, Wanaka
Ph 03 443 1233, Fax 03 443 9238

Lakes Wanaka, Hawea and Surrounding District

■ *Season*

For all rivers and their tributaries flowing into lakes Wanaka and Hawea, 1 November to 31 May. This includes the Makarora, Young, Wilkin, Albert Burn, Matukituki, Hunter, Dingle and Timaru rivers. For lakes Wanaka and Hawea, there is an open season all year.

■ *Restrictions*

The bag limit in these lakes is six fish; for the rivers flowing into Wanaka and Hawea, one fish.

Lake Wanaka

■ *Access*

Road access to many areas of this large lake is somewhat limited and some of the best fishing spots can only be reached by boat. The road to Glendhu Bay and West Wanaka generally follows within walking distance of the shore. SH 6 follows the eastern shore from the head of the lake to the Neck. Aubrey, Beacon Point, Maungawera and Dublin Bay roads give limited access in the vicinity of Wanaka township. There are boat launching facilities at Wanaka, Glendhu Bay and Camp and Wharf Streams up the eastern side of the lake.

Wanaka holds brown and rainbow trout and landlocked quinnat salmon. Most fish are taken by trolling or spinning and fly casting from the shore. Stevensons Arm, the Makarora and Matukituki deltas and Glendhu Bay are good trolling areas. Varieties of Cobra and Toby, Tasmanian Devil, Flatfish and Zed spinners will all take fish. During the winter months use lead line as fish will be feeding on the bottom. A sunk Hamill's Killer is equally effective.

Cruising trout can also be stalked along the shoreline. Paddock Bay, reached from the West Wanaka road via an anglers' access, is a favoured fly fishing area. The bay is

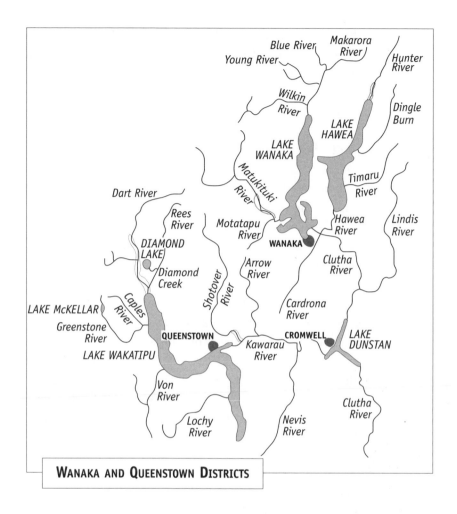

shallow and weedy with sandy patches, and fish cruise in close to the shore. During the day, try a small wet fly or lure such as a Muddler Minnow or Woolly Bugger on a floating line or an unweighted nymph such as Hare's Ear or Pheasant Tail. Cast well ahead of cruising fish or even let your fly sink onto a sandy patch and activate it when a trout cruises within range. At dusk, Dad's Favourite, Kakahi Queen and Twilight Beauty dry flies will all take fish.

If the lake is high, try the shallow inlets near the willows toward the southern end of the bay. Fish cruise close to shore beneath the willows, especially toward dusk. Large cruising fish can usually be viewed from the top of Glendhu Bluff on the roadside near Hell's Gate, but there's no access to the water here. There is good shoreline fly fishing in Stevensons Arm, and even during the winter months fish can be taken on a Hamill's Killer.

LAKE HAWEA
■ *Access*
SH 6 follows the western shore from the Neck to the outlet at Hawea. The private steep and narrow road to Dingle Burn Station follows the eastern shore but generally runs high above the lake. Boat launching facilities are available at the Hawea motor camp.

This lake was raised for power generation, but fishing is still good for browns, rainbows and landlocked quinnat salmon, especially from a boat or by spinning and fly casting from the shore. Hot spots are the Neck, the mouth of Timaru Creek, the Hunter River delta, the Dingle Burn delta and Silver Island. As with Lake Wanaka, cruising trout in the shallower bays can be enticed with flies. There is often good shoreline fishing in winter; try Hamill's Killer, a bully imitation or a Damsel nymph.

HUNTER RIVER
■ *Location and access*
Rises from the Bealey Range of the main divide near the source of the Wills River. From the Forks in the headwaters, the valley follows a southerly direction for 30 km before entering Lake Hawea. Access is usually by jet boat. There is a four-wheel-drive track through the Hunter Valley station to Long Flat Creek, but the owners don't encourage its use as it is risky in all but good weather conditions. There are two fixed wing airstrips in the valley, one at Fergusons Hut and the other near the mouth, but their state of repair varies from time to time. It is a sixteen-hour tramp from Hunter Valley Station to Forbes Hut.

NEW ZEALAND'S TOP TROUT FISHING WATERS

This is a large snow and glacial-fed river flowing down a very long valley. The lower reaches are best fished by spinning or using a downstream lure but there are excellent backwaters where trout can be stalked with a nymph or dry fly.

From Long Flat Creek (Ferguson Hut) to the Forks (Forbes Hut) the river is more confined and stable and there is excellent fly water. Although the river is often milky from glacial flour, both rainbows and browns up to 4 kg can be caught on dry fly, nymph and lure. A Cicada imitation, Humpy, Irresistible and Stimulator fished blindly through pools and fast water can bring surprising results. The valley is exposed to the nor'westers which sweep down with great frequency, frustrating upstream fly anglers. In these conditions it is best to fish downstream with a sunk lure such as Parson's Glory, Yellow Rabbit, Muddler Minnow or Hamill's Killer. At night, using a slow retrieve, try a Hairy Dog or Mrs Simpson in some of the larger holes. Despite being inaccessible, this river deserves its high reputation.

DINGLE BURN

■ *Location and access*
Drains the mountains to the east of Lake Hawea, flows in a southwesterly direction and enters the lake north of Silver Island. Access to the mouth is by boat or by the narrow and scary Timaru River road to Dingle Burn Station. Permission should be obtained from the station when approaching the river from the lower reaches. Tramper-anglers can cross into the upper reaches from the Ahuriri River Valley above Birchwood Station. There's a marked horse track winding up the hill on the south side of the upper Ahuriri River near where the bush starts. Again, permission should be obtained. It is three hours to the Dingle over a high saddle to the upper reaches but the views are magnificent. Many visiting anglers fly in by fixed wing aircraft or helicopter.

This excellent remote stream flowing between high bush-clad mountains is very popular with guides and their clients.

Middle reaches of the Dingle Burn

In the upper reaches, the stream is fast-flowing and narrow and tends to be over-fished. Most fish now seem to have been caught more than once and many are in poor condition. The most accessible water lies between Cotters and the Upper Dingle huts. Here the valley opens out into tussock flats lined by beech forest. The Dingle holds mainly rainbow averaging 1–2 kg in fast-flowing rocky pools and runs. Fish can usually be spotted, but the fast pocket water should not be ignored, especially in warm summer weather. The gorge in the middle reaches is formidable in anything but summer low-water conditions.

A massive flood in December 1995 turned over this lower section and caused severe damage. However, there are some big fish in deep blue pools under the beech bush. Any small weighted nymph or buoyant dry fly should take fish, though some fish have become cunning after having been caught before.

The Dingle Tarn near the mouth of the Dingle Burn on Dingle Burn Station holds brook char (*fontinalis*) with some apparently of trophy size. These are best taken on spinners fished from a boat.

CLUTHA RIVER (UPPER REACHES)
■ *Location and access*
Drains Lake Wanaka and flows south into Lake Dunstan. There are many access points: from Beacon Point Road, off the Dublin Bay road; from Albert Town and Luggate, off SH 6 and SH 8A. A favourite stretch at Deans Bank can be reached from the end of Alison Avenue at Albert Town. In places private farmland needs to be crossed to some of the best water, so please obtain permission. The Upper Clutha Angling Club has published an excellent detailed guide to the Upper Clutha and Lake Dunstan. These are available from Cromwell and Wanaka sports stores.

■ *Season and restrictions*
From the outlet to 600 m above the Albert Town Bridge, 1 October to 31 May, and fly fishing only. Elsewhere, there is an open season all year. Between 600 m above the Albert Town Bridge and the Luggate Bridge, only artificial bait and fly can be used. Below the Luggate Bridge, all legal methods can be used. Bag limit is six fish.

This river has the highest flow rate of any New Zealand river and is not easy to fish. Draining a lake, the upper reaches are stable and remain clear even after heavy rain. There's a very high population of browns and rainbows, especially between the outlet and Albert Town. Drift dives have established that near the outlet this river holds the highest biomass (kg/km) of fish of any New Zealand river (275 fish/km).

During the day, many large fish lie in deep, fast water so it's difficult to get your fly down to these fish. At night, some of these fish feed in the slower-flowing, shallower margins of the current and therefore become accessible to anglers. Sedge fishing on warm summer nights can be most exciting. Use a floating line with a sedge pattern or small wet fly and cast across the current, allowing the fly to swing in towards the shore. Sensitivity is required when fishing this method, so tighten as soon as you feel a strike. If you are late, the deception is rapidly rejected and some takes can be quite vicious. Even 4 kg tippets can be broken.

Trout are not easy to spot but will rise freely late in the evenings during favourable conditions. Fish also respond to a sunk lure such as Woolly Bugger, Mrs Simpson, Hamill's Killer or Yellow Rabbit. At night, try Hairy Dog, Fuzzywuzzy and Marabou patterns but use a 4 kg tippet.

Between Albert Town and the top of Lake Dunstan, the river is large and difficult to fish. However, there is good spin fishing and night sedge fishing at a number of locations. For the spawning run in early winter, try a well-sunk Orange Rabbit or Red Setter, a Glow Bug or Muppet on Tongariro-style gear.

LAKE DUNSTAN

■ *Location and access*

This large hydro lake was formed after the construction of the Clyde Dam. There are two arms — the Kawarau Arm and the Clutha Arm. SH 6 follows the Clutha Arm from Cromwell towards Wanaka. There are marked anglers' accesses off this road. From Tarras to Cromwell SH 8 follows the eastern shoreline of this arm. Access to the less-favoured arm, the Kawarau Arm, is from SH 6 to Queenstown and the bridge to Bannockburn.

■ *Season*
Open all year.

■ *Restrictions*
Bag limit is six fish.

As with most new artificial lakes, the trout (25 000) that were liberated into this lake initially thrived when the surrounding land was first flooded. Despite some decline in the fishing, especially following a severe flood in 1994, there is still reasonable angling in this lake, especially by trolling a spinner or harling a fly from a boat. The lake holds both rainbow and brown trout and landlocked quinnat salmon. In summer, trout can be stalked along the lake edge with a fly, the most productive area being the upper reaches of the Clutha Arm. Try dry flies such as Deer Hair patterns, Humpy, Stimulator, Cicada imitations and Irresistible, lures such as Woolly Bugger, Mrs Simpson and Hamill's Killer and nymphs such as Woolly Caddis, Pheasant Tail and Hare and Copper. A float tube is a decided advantage and enables anglers to fish over weed beds.

In winter, rainbow can be taken on Red Setter and Orange Rabbit lures and Glow Bugs and Muppets. Varieties of Toby, Tasmanian Devil, Gypsy and Cobra are popular for trollers.

QUEENSTOWN DISTRICT

Queenstown, on the shores of Lake Wakatipu, has one of the most spectacular settings in the world. This world-famous tourist destination is renowned for its clear mountain air and long summer twilights. One must take note, however, that mountain weather can be changeable at any time and rapid turns are not uncommon. All major New Zealand airlines provide scheduled daily flights from Auckland, Rotorua, Wellington and Christchurch and return. It is approximately a seven-hour drive from Christchurch and a four-hour excursion from Dunedin.

Queenstown's great outdoors offer a tantalising playground at any time of the year. In winter it is a major ski resort and in the warmer months, aside from the scenic attractions, one can bungy jump, parapent, hang-glide, parachute, jet boat, or raft the whitewater of the Shotover River. For a more peaceful and serene endeavour, a tramp in the Routeburn, Greenstone or Dart valleys would be an option.

There is an intriguing selection of shops, malls, restaurants, bars and nightclubs that cater to every age, taste and budget. In January, for a look at New Zealand lifestyle, the Lake County A & P (agricultural and pastoral) Show and the Glenorchy Races present a wonderful display of New Zealand country living and farming. The Wine, Food and Jazz Festival also held during January is a delightful escape from a day's fishing. A lake cruise on the historic coal-fired steamer *Earnslaw* and a ride on the gondola offer superb views of the lake and the Remarkables. Golfers would be well pleased by the Bob Charles-designed course near Lake Hayes named Millbrook. Train buffs might be interested in a short ride on the historic Kingston Flyer. And for the wine connoisseur there are a number of boutique wineries in the area. For additional retail therapy a stop in Arrowtown would be worthwhile.

Accommodation is not a problem provided it is booked well in advance and the range is broad, from backpackers' hostels to luxury first class hotels.

Fishing gear may be purchased in the city centre sports shop but the discerning angler would be well advised to stock up in Christchurch or Dunedin for specialist equipment. Local professional fly fishing guides are available for hire. If your itinerary does not allow time for a day's fishing in this area perhaps feeding the tame trout off the Queenstown wharf would suffice.

For additional information contact:

Destination Queenstown

PO Box 353, Queenstown

Ph 03 442 7440

Fax 03 442 7441

GREENSTONE AND CAPLES RIVERS

■ *Location and access*

Drain the Livingstone, Ailsa and Humboldt mountains and Lake McKellar. Join 6 km from their mouth and enter the western side of Lake Wakatipu north of Elfin Bay. Access is by boat or south from Kinloch on the rough-metalled Greenstone Station road. There's a parking area at the start of the Greenstone-Caples track at the road end. For the active angler, it is a three-hour tramp from the Divide car park on the Eglinton Road to the McKellar Hut. A further two-hour walk downstream takes you to excellent fishing.

■ *Season*

1 November to 31 May.

■ *Restrictions*
Artificial fly only. Bag limit is one fish.

These are highly regarded and heavily fished scenic mountain rivers holding browns and rainbows up to 4 kg in clear pools and runs. Fishing pressure has increased following road access, so be prepared to tramp upstream to the best water in the middle reaches. There is plenty of good water, with the Greenstone alone offering 30 km of fishable water. The tussock valley is fringed by native bush and is most attractive. The best fishing is in November and December, as many fish will return to Lake Wakatipu by Christmas. However, as with the Lochy and Von rivers, many fish caught early in the season will be mending fish. Thereafter, there will always be resident fish. The Caples Valley is worth visiting for the scenery alone, but the fishing can also be superb, especially early in the season. You will meet plenty of trampers. Try Deer Hair patterns, Humpy, Elk Hair Caddis, Stimulator, Royal Wulff and Green Beetle dry flies; and Green Stonefly, Perla, Hare and Copper and Beadhead nymphs for the deeper holes. The majority of fish are rainbow, but there are some large browns in the deeper holes. Catch and release is recommended.

The mouth offers good lure fishing for running fish late in the season and smelt fly fishing in summer.

VON RIVER

■ *Location and access*
Drains the Thomson Mountains and flows on a northerly course from the branch confluence to enter the western shore of Wakatipu just north of Whites Bay near Mount Nicholas Station. Access is by boat or by road on the Mavora Lakes and Mount Nicholas roads beyond Mavora Lakes.

■ *Season*
1 November to 31 May.

■ *Restrictions*
Artificial fly only. Bag limit is one fish.

A typical West Otago high country stream flowing down a tussock valley, the Von holds in its clear pools and runs browns and rainbows averaging 1.5 kg. It is best fished early in the season, as many fish in the upper reaches will have returned to the lake by Christmas. Fish respond to all methods of fly fishing. Try the same flies as listed for the Greenstone. Fishing has fallen off since road access has become available. The lower gorge can be fished in low-water conditions only, but only active anglers should attempt this. This river valley remains reasonably sheltered in a westerly wind.

The mouth fishes well from April through May.

LOCHY RIVER
■ *Location and access*
Rises in the Eyre Mountains and follows a northeasterly course to enter Lake Wakatipu at Halfway Bay. Access is by boat to the mouth, or by tramping across mountainous tussock country from the Mount Nicholas Road. There is a four-wheel-drive track over Afton Saddle from Mount Nicholas Station and a similar track from Cecil Peak. Permission required.

■ *Season*
1 November to 31 May.

■ *Restrictions*
Fly fishing only in this river. Catch and release upstream from the Long Burn confluence. Below the Long Burn, one fish only may be taken.

The Lochy is another excellent, moderate-sized high country river holding mainly rainbows up to 2.5 kg. There are at least 20 km of fishable water upstream from the mouth. The best water lies above where the Cecil Peak road meets the river,

Lochy River

and fishing continues upstream through a gorge for an hour beyond Killiecrankie Creek. There is a tramping track up the true right bank. The river remains clear after moderate rain and fish are easy to spot. Like the Greenstone, the Lochy is a spawning stream for Lake Wakatipu and many fish return to the lake by Christmas. Use the same flies as for the Greenstone. Overseas anglers may find it easier to access this river by helicopter from Queenstown.

GORE DISTRICT

Gore, in eastern Southland, occupies a strategic position in the southern tourist angler chain with roads radiating west to Fiordland, south to Invercargill and east to the rugged Catlin Coast. The excellence of its brown trout fishing has given Southland a worldwide reputation and Gore lays claim to being the 'Brown Trout Capital of the World'. Gore, a moderate-sized country town, is a one-hour drive from Invercargill, a two-and-a-quarter-hour ride from Dunedin and a two-hour journey from Te Anau.

On non-fishing days we suggest visiting Invercargill and the Southland Museum to watch live tuatara, attending Tulip International in the spring or early summer, taking a vintage aircraft flight from Mandeville or looking at the porcelain dolls at the Dollsmiths in Mataura. There are respectable golf clubs in Gore, Mataura and Invercargill.

Accommodation is adequate with motels, hotels, home-stays and camping grounds. We would suggest a farmstay to better acquaint yourself with the local customs.

Fishing guides are available for hire in Gore and the sports shops have adequate supplies of fly fishing equipment.

For further information contact one of the following:
* Gore Information Centre, Ordsal Street, Gore
  Phone and fax 03 208 9908
* Tourism Southland, PO Box 903, Invercargill
  Ph 03 214 9733
  Fax 03 218 9460

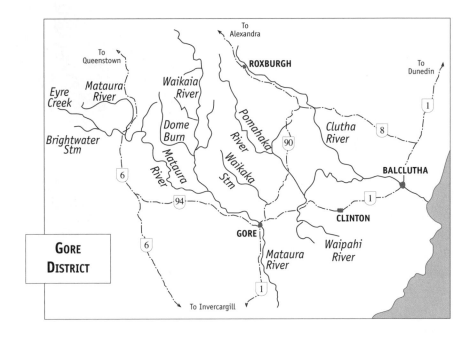

MATAURA RIVER AND TRIBUTARIES

MATAURA RIVER

■ *Location and access*

Rises from the Eyre and Garvie mountains south of Lake Wakatipu. Follows a southeasterly course to Gore where it turns and flows south to finally empty into Toetoes Bay at Fortrose.

■ *Season*

Below the Gorge Road traffic bridge on SH 92, the river is open all year. Elsewhere, 1 October–30 April.

■ *Restrictions*

Bag limit upstream from the Black Bridge at Athol is four fish; above Garston bridge catch and release is to be practised; elsewhere the bag limit is six fish.

This famous brown trout river provides about 150 km of easy fishable water. For convenience, the river is divided into three sections:

Upper Mataura River

Upper Mataura (Fairlight to Cattle Flat)
■ *Access*

Access above Garston from SH 6 is across private farmland and permission must be obtained. There are fish upstream as far as Fairlight. Between Garston and Athol the river is small, willow-lined and flows over farmland. Access is not a problem, but again ask permission before crossing private land. Below Parawa, a shingle road running east gives good access to the Nokomai Gorge.

There are reasonable stocks of brown trout in the 0.75–1.2 kg range which can be spotted under bright, low-water conditions in summer. However, the water is a greenish-grey colour and fish are difficult to see when the river runs above normal. There are miles of good fishing water, even right down through the Nokomai Gorge (40 fish/km at Nokomai on drift dives, with 40 percent a good size), and the river is easily crossed at the tail of most pools, although the stones tend to be slippery.

Even during cold conditions during early spring, there is often a good rise on the Mataura River. Mayflies and caddis form the bulk of the trout's diet so try Dad's Favourite, Black

Quill Gnat, Twilight Beauty, Kakahi Queen, Dark Red Spinner, Blue Dun, Compara-Dun, Elk Hair Caddis and Adams Parachute dry flies in sizes 14–18. Sunk Pheasant Tail and Hare's Ear nymphs take fish as will March Brown, Purple Grouse and Twilight Beauty wet flies. On warm summer evenings when fish are rising vigorously, try a Caddis imitation or a sparsely tied wet fly fished sensitively upstream or across and down on a floating line. Even a Hairy Dog, Fuzzywuzzy or Mrs Simpson fished deep through the pools after dark can be rewarding.

Middle reaches (Cattle Flat down to Gore)

■ *Access*

There are many access points, including from the Ardlussa-Cattle Flat Road, Ardlussa bridge, Waipounamu bridge, Pyramid bridge at Riversdale, Mandeville, Otamita bridge, Monaghans Beach at Croydon and Graham's Island at Gore.

This is the most popular stretch of river. The river is slower-flowing, grass- and willow-lined and meanders across farmland. It becomes a large river below the Waikaia confluence and fording is hazardous. Fish are difficult to spot unless rising or cruising the backwaters, but stocks are high, especially below the Waikaia. Use the same methods as outlined for the Upper Mataura with the addition of willow grub imitation in December and January. During the 'mad rise' try small emergers. If fish are quietly rising, try spent spinners such as Owaka or Houghtons Ruby in sizes 16–18. If the river is high and discoloured, try spinning with an Articulated Trout, Veltic or Devon.

The Tomogalak Stream entering the Mataura north of Balfour is worth investigating early in the season.

Lower Mataura (Gore to the mouth)

■ *Access*

There's good road access to many well-known fishing spots on the lower Mataura.

The river is larger and deeper and water quality deteriorates, especially below Mataura Island. Fish cannot be spotted, but they are prolific. At times the 'mad Mataura rise' can be totally frustrating. Use the same flies and methods as already described, but a small unweighted dark nymph fished upstream can bring results when all else fails.

Below Mataura Island the river becomes less attractive but still provides good fishing, especially in the stretch from Wyndham down to Gorge Road bridge on SH 92 at the top of the tidal section. Live bait methods are popular in this stretch.

BRIGHTWATER STREAM
■ *Location and access*
This small, clear, weedy, spring-fed stream flows across private farmland just south of Fairlight. Take Fairlight Station road off SH 6 and please ask permission from the landowner before fishing.

Use 'spring creek' flies such as small Pheasant Tail and Hare and Copper nymphs, Midge Pupa, Mayfly and Caddis emergers and small dry Mayfly patterns. The fish are a good size and very shy, so a careful approach and fine tippets are essential. This is an important spawning stream but, being spring-fed, it does not colour during a fresh. Wading is unnecessary and only disturbs the stream bed. Avoid spooking fish by fishing when the light is bright. Carry a landing net. Hooked fish often escape into weed.

WAIKAIA RIVER
■ *Location and access*
Like the Pomahaka River, the Waikaia rises in the Umbrella Mountains of Central Otago. It flows in a southerly direction for over 50 km to join the Mataura River at Riversdale. Access is readily available from the Riversdale, Waikaia and Piano Flat roads. There is a four-wheel-drive track beyond Piano Flat.

■ *Season and restrictions*
Below Niagara Bridge the river is open all year. Above this bridge, 1 October–30 April. Above Glenray Bridge the bag limit is four fish; elsewhere, six fish.

This moderate-sized, highly regarded brown trout river is the Mataura's major tributary. The inaccessible upper reaches above Piano Flat flow down a picturesque beech-clad valley but only hold a few fish. However, if one is prepared to walk then there are a few good deep holes up as far as Whitecoomb Flats 10 km or so upstream from Piano Flat (40 fish/km on drift dives at Piano Flat).

The middle and lower reaches with their willow-lined banks and shingle bed wind across farmland. In clear, bright conditions, fish can be spotted and angled for despite the lightly tea-coloured water. But stocks are sufficiently great that 'blind' fly fishing can be most rewarding.

There are long pools and runs, access is good and the river can be safely waded. There is excellent water at Argyle Road. It holds fish in the 0.75–1.5 kg range. A wide selection of flies will take fish; try Dad's Favourite, Twilight Beauty, Blue Dun, Dark Red Spinner and Red Quill Gnat dry flies, Pheasant Tail, Hare's Ear and Half Back nymphs or Hardy's Favourite, March Brown, Purple Grouse and Twilight Beauty wet flies. A willow grub imitation can be deadly. There is often a good caddis hatch on warm summer evenings.

Early in the season, Dome Burn at Waikaia and Steeple Burn 7 km further upstream are worth exploring. They are both spawning streams which can remain fishable when the main river is discoloured.

POMAHAKA RIVER

■ *Location and access*
Rises in the Umbrella Mountains south of Roxburgh and winds for 125 km through West Otago to enter the Clutha below Clydevale not far from the mouth of the Waiwera River. There's good road access to most of the river.

■ Season
1 October–30 April.

■ *Restrictions*
Bag limit above Park Hill Bridge is three fish; below this
bridge, six fish.

Upper Pomahaka (above Switzers or Park Hill Bridge)
■ *Access*
From roads northeast of Kelso, Tapanui and Heriot. Take Old
Switzers road to Park Hill Domain, Hukarere Station Road,
Spylaw Burn Road or Aitcheson's Runs Road to Hamiltons
Flat.

The river meanders across attractive but exposed barren
tussock country. There are some deep pools, but the water is
clear-flowing over a rock-and-stone bed and fish can be
spotted. Although their run is unpredictable, large sea-run
browns from the Clutha weighing up to 4.5 kg arrive in this
area to spawn during February to March. They respond to
sunk nymphs, dry flies and black lures fished deep through
the holes after dark.

Middle and lower reaches
■ *Access middle*
From the Waipehi-Conical Hill road which parallels the river
near the Conical Hill sawmill. The Waikoikoi Road crosses
between Tapanui and Conical Hill.

■ *Access lower*
From Burkes Ford Road, Ross Road, Taumata Road, Clinton-
Clydevale Road and the Waiwera-Clydevale Road at Black's
Bridge.

The water is variable in these sections. Dusky Forest offers
rough boots-and-shorts fishing. Between Kelso and Tapanui
the river enters a fishable gorge; from Tapanui to Conical
Hill, it winds across farmland and becomes willow-lined,

weedy, slower-flowing, holding fish averaging 1.2 kg. Downstream from Conical Hill the river soon becomes swift and the banks are choked with willows, and fish cannot be spotted in the peat-coloured water. There are stretches of water that can be fished; however, the middle reaches are the most heavily fished, with many anglers preferring to spin. The lower reaches are slow-flowing and deep and although fly anglers catch fish, many use live bait and spinners.

WAIPAHI RIVER

■ *Location and access*
Rises from swampy tussock country west of Clinton and winds its way across open swampy farmland generally in a northerly direction to join the Pomahaka River south of Conical Hill. SH 1 crosses the river at Arthurton and Webb Road off SH 1 leads to the lower reaches. The Clinton-Gore back road crosses higher up while the road to Wyndham leaves from this crossing and generally follows the river upstream.

The Waipahi is highly regarded as a fly stream holding browns averaging around 1 kg and fishes best early and late in the season, as weed growth from eutrophication causes problems in high summer.

Fish are not easy to spot in the slightly tea-coloured water so blind fishing the runs or fishing to rising fish is advised. At the end of October there's a local annual fishing competition — the Gold Medal Event — on this river. Try Hare and Copper and Pheasant Tail nymphs, Midge Pupa imitation or Dad's Favourite, Kakahi Queen and Greenwell's Dark dry flies in sizes 16–18. Emerger patterns and No Hackle Dun also take fish.

Other rivers worth fishing in the Gore vicinity include the Otamita, Otapiri and Mimihau.

TE ANAU AND FIORDLAND DISTRICT

The hub of Fiordland is the small tourist town of Te Anau nestled on the edge of Lake Te Anau. Fiordland National Park is a World Heritage Park and during high summer, busloads of tourists pass through Te Anau en route to Milford Sound or to walk the Milford Track, touted to be the most beautiful walk in the world. As Te Anau lies on the edge of Fiordland its rainfall is considerably less than the 6000–8000 mm per year that parts of Fiordland experience. However, the weather can be cool and unsettled, especially in the spring. February and March are the warmest and driest months.

Fiordland National Park offers scenery that is unsurpassed in the world: towering snowcapped mountains, dense native bush, shimmering lakes, sheer rock walls, cascading waterfalls and deep black fiords. A scenic flight over this area on a clear day is an unforgettable experience as is a boat trip on Milford or Doubtful Sound. Other scenic sensations include the glow worm caves, the newly developed underwater seaquarium in Milford Sound, the underground Manapouri Power House (the west arm of Lake Manapouri), and a drive up the Eglinton Valley to Milford via the historic Homer Tunnel.

There are tours of all descriptions ranging from Bird and Bush, Photo, and Ecology Holidays to guided walks and tramps. For the fit tramper, the Kepler, Milford, Greenstone, Routeburn and Hollyford tracks will satisfy any lover of glorious wilderness country. We advise you to call the Fiordland National Park Visitor Centre for additional details

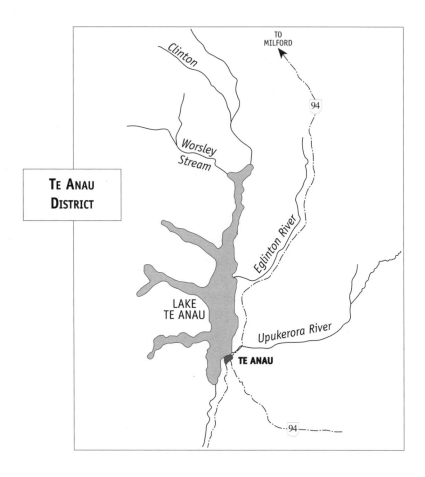

TE ANAU
DISTRICT

and weather updates. Golfers will enjoy the Te Anau course along the shores of the lake.

Accommodation caters to every budget with a luxury hotel, motels, lodges, guest houses, bed and breakfasts, farmstays, a youth hostel, cabins, backpackers' hostel and motor camps. It is wise to book ahead in this tourist resort. Although Te Anau is a small town there are a surprising number of restaurants that will please even the most discerning palate. And, fresh crayfish can be purchased at the Key (a 20-minute drive from Te Anau).

The sports shop in town has an adequate supply of fly fishing tackle and there are a number of professional fly fishing guides available for hire.

For more information contact one of the following:
- Fiordland Travel Centre, PO Box 1, Te Anau
  Ph 03 249 8900
- Tourism Southland, PO Box 903, Invercargill
  Ph 03 214 9733
  Fax 03 218 9460

LAKE TE ANAU AND RELATED WATERS

CLINTON RIVER

■ *Location and access*

Rises near the Mackinnon Pass on the Milford Track, flows southeast and enters the head of Lake Te Anau at Glade House. Access is by boat from Te Anau Downs or Te Anau, or by tramping a very difficult route over Dore Pass from the Eglinton Valley. The Milford Track follows the river upstream.

Camping is permitted in the north branch only and not in the main Clinton Valley. Please obtain permission from the Department of Conservation, Te Anau.

■ *Season*

1 November to 31 May.

■ *Restrictions*

The bag limit is two fish. Artificial bait only.

This is a magnificent river holding browns and rainbows up to 4 kg in gin-clear water. Fish are very shy, but a cautious approach, accurate casting and a long, fine trace so as not to line the fish will bring results. The river flows through heavy bush and is littered with sunken logs brought down in floods.

Fish can be taken on well-sunk nymphs and dry flies but one or two fish a day is really good going. It seldom remains fine in this high-rainfall area for more than three days on end but the river rarely discolours. Insect repellent is essential.

The North Branch, Neale Burn and Lake Ross all hold trout and offer good fishing for the tramper-angler.

WORSLEY STREAM

■ *Location and access*

Drains lakes Sumor and Brownlee, flows on an easterly course and enters the top end of Te Anau at Worsley Arm. Access by boat or floatplane.

■ Season

1 November to 31 May.

■ *Restrictions*

Bag limit is two fish.

This remote and scenic river flows through rugged, bush-covered, mountainous terrain, the habitat of wapiti herds, and holds browns and rainbows, the latter predominating. Fish up to 4 kg can be taken using similar fishing methods as for the Clinton. This is high quality fishing water. Good fishing is available to beyond the Castle confluence and in the lower reaches of the Castle. The Parks Board hut near the mouth of the Worsley is heavily used, especially during

Worsley Stream rainbow

weekends and holidays. The track up the true left bank has become overgrown and is washed out in some sections. The lower Worsley is best accessed by boat.

There are a number of clear mountain streams entering the western side of Lake Te Anau which are well worth fishing, with access being by boat or floatplane. All the streams drain steep, heavily bushed country and anglers need to combine tramping with angling. Such streams are the Glaisnock River entering the head of the North Fiord, the Lugar Burn also entering the North Fiord, the Doon River entering the southwest arm of the Middle Fiord and the Ettrick Burn entering the lake just north of the Te Anau Glow Worm Caves.

EGLINTON RIVER

■ *Location and access*
Flows into and out of lakes Fergus and Gunn, then down the scenic Eglinton Valley, following a southerly direction, to enter Lake Te Anau north of Te Anau Downs. There is road access to the mouth from Te Anau Downs. SH 94 follows the river upstream on its true left bank, although a walk across tussock flats and through beech bush is sometimes necessary to reach the river.

■ *Season*
1 November to 31 May.

■ *Restrictions*
Fly fishing only. The bag limit is two fish. Between Waterfall and Smithy creeks, catch and release only.

This excellent river has easy access to clear water containing mainly rainbow but also a few brown trout. Fish can be spotted in clear, bright conditions and taken on dry flies, nymphs and sunk lures. There are well-defined pools and runs and the river can be crossed and waded in selected places and at the tail of most pools. The river bed is shingly and the banks covered with grass, scrub and patches of beech bush. Snow melt can keep the river high until December. Fishing is best during periods of low flow.

The lower and middle reaches around Walker and Mackay creeks tend to hold most fish, though trout can be caught up as far as Cascade Creek. There is good water below Knob's Flat and some large fish are present in the gorge. This is an important spawning river for Lake Te Anau.

The east branch is unstable in the lower reaches, but reasonable fishing can be obtained if one is prepared to tramp and scramble for three hours upstream. The access track is marked near the road bridge.

Upukerora River

■ *Location and access*

Rises in the Livingstone Mountains and flows on a southwesterly course through farmland to enter Lake Te Anau at Patience Bay just north of Te Anau township. Access to the lower reaches is from SH 94 3 km north of the township where the road crosses the river. Walk upstream from the bridge. The middle and upper reaches can be reached from Kakapo Road which leaves SH 94 5 km south of Te Anau. Turn left off Kakapo Road onto Ladies' Mile Road; there is an anglers' access through private land to the river. The end of Kakapo Road leads to the upper reaches through private farmland. Please ask permission.

■ *Season*

1 November to 31 May.

■ *Restrictions*

Fly fishing only. Bag limit is two fish.

An important spawning stream for Lake Te Anau, this river can dry somewhat during hot summer conditions. The Upukerora holds mainly rainbow with an odd brown, especially late in the season and in the upper reaches. Although close to Te Anau, there is a good population of fish in this river, wading is easy on a shingle bed and the pools and ripples are a delight to fish. Fish are easily seen and although scary in low-water conditions they will accept dry flies and nymphs carefully presented. This river is ideal for the learner fly fisher and catch and release is recommended. The mouth is worth fishing at night, providing the stream is not too braided.

LAKE TE ANAU

■ *Season*
Open all year.

■ *Restrictions*
Bag limit is four fish.

This is the largest lake in the South Island, being 61 km long and covering 850 ha. The western shore is broken up into fiords which penetrate deep into the rugged bush-covered Fiordland mountains. The eastern shore is drier, grass-covered and farmed.

The lake is best fished by trolling from a boat or spinning from the shore though there are a few selected spots, mainly at stream mouths, where fly anglers can fish. Fish are hard to see except at shallow deltas such as the Eglinton. There is good shoreline fishing at the golf course. Night lure fishing at stream mouths can be excellent. The lake contains rainbow and brown trout along with a few landlocked Atlantic salmon. The lake level is controlled at the outlet by a weir.

WHITESTONE RIVER

■ *Location and access*
Rises from the Livingstone Mountains to the west of Mavora Lakes, flows on a southerly course and joins the lower reaches of the Mararoa River south of the Manapouri road in the Mount York area. Access from the Hillside-Manapouri road to the lower reaches, from SH 94 (Lumsden-Te Anau road) to the middle reaches and from Kakapo Road off SH 94 and through private farmland to the upper reaches.

Billy tea

■ *Season*
1 October to 30 April.

■ *Restrictions*
Bag limit is two fish.

This small stream draining the Snowden State Forest and flowing through pastoral land tends to dry in summer, though there are still some good pools in the middle and upper reaches that can be fished even when the river is very low at the SH 94 bridge. It holds small numbers of good-sized browns and rainbows which can be stalked in clear conditions. Fish spawn in this river and many drop back downstream by December. Some trout caught early in the season will still be recovering from spawning. There are always resident fish in the middle and lower reaches.

MARAROA RIVER

■ *Location*

Rises between the Livingstone and Thomson mountains just south of Greenstone Valley and flows south down a barren tussock valley and into North Mavora Lake. Drains this lake and enters the bush-clad South Mavora Lake 4 km further south. Emerges from South Mavora and continues through bush for 3 km before the valley opens out into tussock and farmland. The river becomes braided in this section, then flows in a southerly direction for over 40 km before joining the Whitestone River south of the Hillside-Manapouri road. After flowing through a gorge, the river joins the Waiau 6.5 km south of Lake Manapouri just above the weir.

■ *Season*

1 October to 30 April.

■ *Restrictions*

Bag limit is four fish below Key Bridge and two fish above. Artificial bait and fly only above Key Bridge.

Upper reaches

■ *Access*

The top end of North Mavora Lake can be reached by boat and by a four-wheel-drive on a rough track along the eastern side of the lake. Between the two lakes and downstream from the South Mavora outlet, there is access off the Te Anau-Mavora Lakes road.

The Upper Mararoa River runs through a very exposed tussock valley. There is good sight fishing for browns and rainbows for 8 km above North Mavora Lake. These must be approached with care — the fish are easily spooked and there are deep holes between the tussocks. The Windon Burn entering the Mararoa from the west also holds a few good fish in the lower pools, especially early and late in the season. There are usually a few fish between the two lakes, where the water is deep, clear and fast-flowing.

Middle reaches
■ *Access*

SH 94 crosses the river just beyond the Key. Turn off SH 94 at Burwood Station onto the Te Anau-Mavora Lakes road, which leads upstream on the true left bank to South Mavora Lake. The Centre Hill-Mavora Lakes road, also off SH 94, joins this road at the apex of a triangle. There are marked access points for anglers off the Te Anau-Mavora Lakes road and at the Mararoa Station bridge.

At the southern end of South Mavora Lake, the river is stable for 3 km and flows through bush and tussock on a rock-and-stone bed. This is a superb river, holding trout in the 1.2–3 kg range (25 large fish/km on drift dives). Above Kiwi Burn, 70 percent of fish are rainbow; below Wood Burn, 70 percent of fish are browns. Do not be fooled by first impressions as although much of the water downstream from the bush is braided and looks unstable, it holds good stocks of fish which can be spotted in summer, low-water conditions. Fishing can be difficult when the river is high, as crossings can be hazardous and the stones are very slippery. The water remains fishable after rain but the catch rate falls off. Try Stimulator, Royal Wulff and Humpy dry flies in the rough water in sizes 8–12; Twilight Beauty, Dad's Favourite, Greenwell's Glory and Coch-y-bondhu in the calmer stretches in sizes 12–16; Mrs Simpson, Woolly Bugger and Muddler Minnow lures and any well-weighted nymph, especially when the river is high. Two beadheads may be necessary in these conditions.

Nor'west winds can be a problem for the upstream fly angler but there is more shelter in the stretch of river above Kiwi Burn.

Lower reaches
■ *Access*

Weir Road from Manapouri follows the Waiau River and crosses the Mararoa River below its gorge and near the weir.

Flood damage on a West Coast river

There's reasonable fishing above this bridge and upstream through the gorge for the active boots-and-shorts angler but only when the river is low. Higher upstream, at the Hillside-Manapouri road bridge over the Whitestone River, look for a track on the left 1.5 km further down the road towards Manapouri. This leads downstream to the Whitestone confluence, Flaxy Creek and the top end of the gorge. There are usually a few fish in the lower reaches of Flaxy Creek. The Mararoa in this area is braided, shingly, and willow-lined. Although more difficult to fish, there are good-sized trout in this section.

MAVORA LAKES
■ *Location and access*
Lie between the Livingstone and Thomson mountains just south and west of Lake Wakatipu. From SH 94 take the branch roads to Mavora Lakes from either Centre Hill or

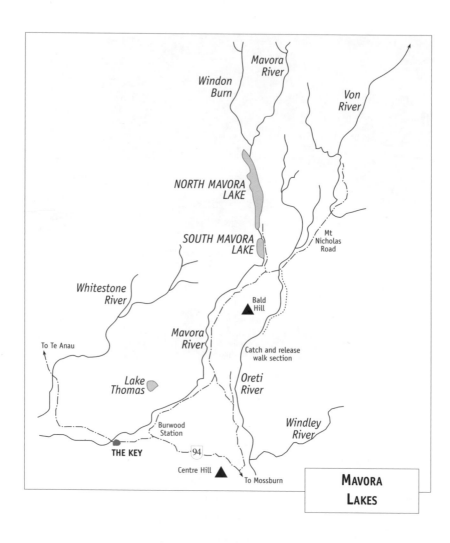

Burwood Station. These roads join and follow up the Mararoa River to the lakes.

■ *Season*
1 October to 30 April.

■ *Restrictions*
Artificial bait only and the bag limit is two trout.

North Mavora is 9.5 km long and except for patches of beech bush near the southern end is surrounded by tussock and matagouri-covered mountains. There's a very rough four-wheel-drive track up the east side of the lake to the head. Rainbow and brown trout can be spotted cruising the lake margins and will accept dry flies, nymphs and small lures. The eastern and northern shoreline are favoured spots. Fish are also taken on spinners and by trolling. The lake has deteriorated as a fishery since the road was built twenty years ago and boats were introduced, but fish still average 1.6 kg.

At 2.5 km in length, South Mavora is a smaller lake and being surrounded by native bush is more sheltered. There's good fly fishing for cruising trout round the lake margin and in the shallow inlets, especially at the northern end where the river enters. Camping sites with minimal facilities are available. The lakes are worth visiting for their scenic beauty alone but the tranquillity may be disturbed during the Christmas holiday season by trail bikes and power boats.

ORETI RIVER AND TRIBUTARIES
ORETI RIVER
■ *Location and access*
Rises in the Thomson Mountains just east of North Mavora Lake and flows south for over 130 km before entering the New River Estuary at Invercargill.

■ *Season*
Open all year downstream from the Riverton/Invercargill Highway. Elsewhere, 1 October–30 April.

■ *Restrictions*
Between Lincoln Hill and the Mount Nicholas bridge, all fish caught must be released. Above Mossburn (Rocky Point is signposted), the bag limit is two fish and only artificial bait is permitted. Below Rocky Point the bag limit is six fish.

For convenience, the river is divided into sections:

Upper reaches (above Mossburn)

■ *Access*

SH 94 follows the river from Mossburn to the Mavora Lakes turnoff. The Centre Hill-Mavora Lakes road then follows the river upstream but leaves it when it passes on the west side of Bald Hill. There are marked anglers' access tracks off the Centre Hill-Mavora Lakes road. A small side road, the Oreti Rd, leads to a gate and the upper reaches. This is a walk-wade, catch and release section. The Mount Nicholas road crosses the Upper Oreti 2 km after leaving the Mavora Lakes road (see Mavora Lakes map).

Between Lincoln Hill and the Mount Nicholas bridge there is good fly fishing for some very large fish. However, fish stocks in the first 3 km downstream from the bridge are not high. The catch rate is much higher in the 10 km upstream of the Oreti Road. As these are resident fish, they must be carefully returned after landing. The river winds across exposed tussock flats and has a shingle bed.

Trout can be spotted and stalked, but the prevailing nor'wester can seriously frustrate the upstream fly angler. Trophy fish can be caught in this section but the fish are shy and sophisticated and will only be deceived by expert fly presentation. When frightened, they dive for cover under the tussock banks.

Early in the season, try well-weighted mayfly or caddis nymphs on a long fine tippet. On hot summer days try Humpy, Stimulator, Cicada, Elk Hair Caddis, Hoppers, Coch-y-bondhu and Royal Wulff dry flies in sizes 10–14. If the wind prevents upstream fishing, try floating a nymph or cicada on a long trace down with the current to fish you can see — it is helpful to have a mate spotting for you when using this technique. If this fails, a Muddler Minnow or Woolly Bugger swung across the current on a slow sinking line may very occasionally prove successful.

Just above Mossburn, 60 fish/km have been counted on

drift dives, half of which are good-sized fish.

The Windley River tributary entering the true left bank below Coal Hill and the Weydon Burn at Centre Hill are worth a look early in the season. SH 94 follows the Weydon Burn.

Middle reaches (Mossburn to Centre Bush)

■ *Access*

Between Mossburn and Lumsden from SH 94. Between Lumsden and Centre Bush there are numerous marked anglers' access tracks from both banks off SH 6 and the Dipton-Mossburn road.

The river in this section is occasionally willow-lined though more often the banks are open and exposed, with the river somewhat braided. It flows over an unstable shingle bed, but there are good long glides and riffles. Fish are difficult to spot, so fish blind with Dad's Favourite, Adams, Coch-y-bondhu or Royal Wulff dry flies, Pheasant Tail and Olive nymphs or March Brown wet flies, all in the smaller sizes. Fish stocks are good.

Lower reaches (from Centre Bush bridge to the Invercargill-Riverton SH 99 roadbridge)

Below Winton the river is slower-flowing and willow-lined, with mud banks. Spinning and live-bait fishing become more effective, although fish can still be taken on flies. It holds good stocks of smaller fish in the 0.5–1 kg range.

About the Authors

John Kent, a retired medical practitioner, was born and raised in Christchurch but has lived in both the North and the South Island. John has held a New Zealand trout fishing licence for the past 48 years and has tramped and fished extensively throughout both islands. His first book, *North Island Trout Fishing Guide*, was published by Reed Publishing in 1989. The *South Island Trout Fishing Guide* followed one year later. Both books have been reprinted and updated. In addition, John has written 26 short stories for *Rod and Rifle* magazine. In 1996–97, John fished in Montana and Alaska and was a guest speaker at the International Federation of Flyfishers (FFF) Conclave in Livingston, Montana, and Grand Rapids, Michigan. He has been invited again to address the FFF Conclave in Idaho Falls, Idaho, in 1998.

Patti Magnano Madsen is a full-time flyfisher living six months in Great Falls, Montana and six months in Christchurch, New Zealand. She has been actively involved with the International Federation of Fly Fishers (FFF) for several years as a demonstration fly tier and as an instructor for fly tying workshops and Mel Krieger's casting clinics. She is a certified flycasting instructor and has taught in many states in the USA as well as in Canada, New Zealand and Argentina. Patti is also a member of the Montana Professional Guides Association. She has been 'trouting' in New Zealand for the past ten years and spends 300 days annually in pursuit of the ever-elusive brown and rainbow trout. When not fishing Montana or New Zealand waters she can be found casting flies in Alaska, Canada and South America.

INDEX